# Essential
# iPad
## iOS 12 Edition

## Kevin Wilson

Elluminet Press
www.elluminetpress.com

# Essential iPad: iOS 12 Edition

Publisher: Elluminet Press
Director: Kevin Wilson
Lead Editor: Steven Ashmore
Technical Reviewer: Mike Taylor, Robert Ashcroft
Copy Editors: Joanne Taylor, James Marsh
Proof Reader: Mike Taylor
Indexer: James Marsh
Cover Designer: Kevin Wilson

eBook versions and licenses are also available for most titles. Any source code or other supplementary materials referenced by the author in this text is available to readers at

www.elluminetpress.com/resources

For detailed information about how to locate your book's resources, go to

www.elluminetpress.com/resources

# Table of Contents

# About the Author

Kevin Wilson has made a career out of technology and showing others how to use it. After earning a master's degree in computer science, software engineering, and multimedia systems, Kevin worked as a tutor and college instructor, helping students master such subjects as multimedia, computer literacy and information technology. He currently serves as Elluminet Press Publishing's senior writer and director, he periodically teaches computing at college in South Africa and serves as an IT trainer in England.

Kevin's motto is clear: "If you can't explain something simply, you haven't understood it well enough." To that end, he has created the Computer Essentials series, in which he breaks down complex technological subjects into smaller, easy-to-follow steps that students and ordinary computer users can put into practice.

# Acknowledgements

Thanks to all the staff at Luminescent Media & Elluminet Press for their passion, dedication and hard work in the preparation and production of this book.

To all my friends and family for their continued support and encouragement in all my writing projects.

To all my colleagues, students and testers who took the time to test procedures and offer feedback on the book

Finally thanks to you the reader for choosing this book. I hope it helps you to use your iPad with greater ease.

# Chapter 1

# iOS 12

iOS is a mobile, multitasking operating system designed specifically for iPads and iPhones. iOS 12 is the latest release for iPhones and iPads.

An Operating System is a program that manages the device's hardware resources such as memory, processor and storage. The Operating System also provides a platform for you to run apps such as web browsers, maps, email, photos, games and so on.

The iOS user interface is a touch screen, meaning you can directly manipulate sliders, switches, buttons and icons on screen using your finger.

iOS has a main screen called the home screen containing icons that represent apps. You can download countless apps from the App Store - you'll find an app for almost anything you can think of.

Security has improved on these devices, you can unlock just with a finger print - no need to keep remembering a PIN.

Finally there's Siri, the voice activated personal assistant that uses natural language AI to interpret voice commands you speak out loud. You can ask Siri to send messages, dial a number, as well as search the web, and answer certain questions.

# What's New?

With iOS 12, Apple have concentrated on improving performance - meaning apps load faster, and are generally more responsive.

iBooks has been renamed Apple Books and makes it easier to find and read your ebooks.

Apple News app has been redesigned, making it easier to keep up with the news that interests you.

The control center has been moved and you can now find it by swiping downwards from the top right hand edge of the screen.

Apple have introduced voice memos to the iPad, so you can record notes right from your iPad.

# Chapter 1: iOS 12

Screen Time is a new feature that allows you to keep track of your iPad usage, as well as giving you stats and reports on your child's online activity

There is also a new augmented reality measure app that allows you to measure distances - still not quite as accurate as a tape measure but it isn't bad.

FaceTime has also had a few updates. You can now talk to multiple people using Group FaceTime, as well as liven up your chat using various camera effects.

A couple of new navigation touch gestures to take note of. Now you can return to the home screen by simply swiping upward from the bottom edge of the screen. Reveal your app switcher by swiping from the bottom edge to the center of the screen.

Also in the mix are new ways to share photos, Siri has a few new shortcuts, as well as the usual security tweaks and other enhancements.

**Chapter 2**

# Setting up Your iPad

If you've just bought your new iPad and taken it out the box, the process to set it up to use for the first time is very simple. You don't even have to connect it to your computer.

With iOS 12, Apple have dropped support for the iPad 2, so iOS 12 can only be installed on the following devices.

- iPad Pro 1st & 2nd generation
- iPad 6th generation
- iPad 5th generation
- iPad Air 2
- iPad Air
- iPad mini 4
- iPad mini 3
- iPad mini 2
- iPhone X, 8, 7, 6, SE, & 5S

iOS 12 is compatible with 64-bit devices only, so the iPhone 5, iPhone 5c, and iPad 2 do not support the software update. So if you're upgrading your iPad, keep this in mind.

In this section we'll take a look at the processes of setting up your iPad when you turn it on for the first time.

# Insert your SIM

**Make sure your device is off before doing this.** If your iPad has a SIM card or you're using an iPhone, you'll need to insert your SIM card from your network provider.

Push the end of a paper clip into the release hole on the side of your device. Pull out the little tray and insert your SIM.

Nano SIM Size

Micro SIM Size

Std SIM Size

Slide the little tray back into your device, until it fits firmly into place against the side.

You're now ready to power on your iPad. To do this, hold down the power button located on the top of your device, until you see the Apple logo on the screen.

Give your iPad a few seconds to start up.

# Power Up & Power Down

Once your iPad battery is fully charged, press and hold the power button for a couple of seconds until you see the apple logo.

To completely shut down your iPad, press and hold the power button for a few seconds, until you see the shut down slider on your screen. Slide your finger across the slider to shut down your iPad.

slide to power off

It's a good a idea to completely power down your iPad from time to time to reset its resources - this can help when your iPad seems to be running slower than usual. Most of the time your iPad goes into sleep mode when in normal use.

# Unlock & Wake iPad

The home button also contains a finger print scanner and is usually set up during the initial setup.

Place your finger on the button so your thumb fits snugly into the button's indent, then press the button once to unlock your iPad - **don't** hold the button down.

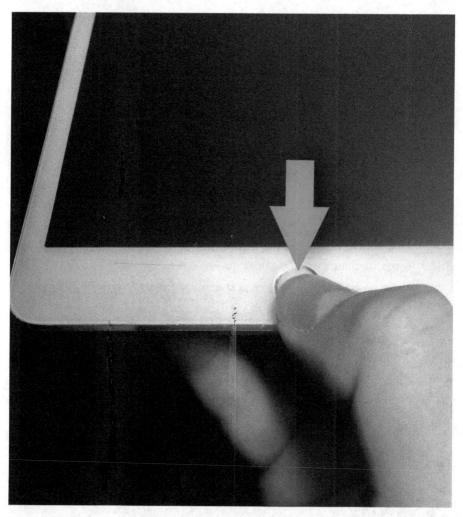

If you haven't set up your finger print scanner, you'll be prompted for your passcode. This is the code you enter during the initial setup procedure.

# Force Shutdown

Sometimes your iPad can become unresponsive or freeze. When this happens you can force a shutdown.

To do this, hold down the power button on the top, and the home button at the same time until the screen goes blank.

Once the screen has gone blank, wait a few seconds, then press and hold the power button for a couple of seconds, until the apple logo appears on screen.

Your iPad will start up.

# Upgrading your iPad to iOS 12

Make sure your iPad is plugged into a power charger and that it is connected to your WiFi.

Once you have done that, go to the settings app and tap 'General', then select 'Software Update'.

Tap 'Download and Install'.

To update now, tap 'download and install'. Enter your passcode when prompted. Your iPad will restart and the update will install. This might take a while.

# Initial Setup

To use iPad, you need an internet connection and your Apple ID. For iOS 11 & iOS 12, Apple have introduced an automated setup feature that allows you to transfer settings from another device, such as an iPhone. Both devices must be running iOS 11 or iOS 12. If you don't have this, you can still set up your iPad manually. First lets take a look at the auto setup feature.

## Auto Setup

If you have iOS11 or iOS12 set up on another device such as an iPhone, you can use it to transfer your settings to your new iPad.

On your iPad, slide or press the home button to start, then select your language

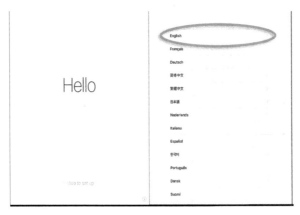

Select your region or country.

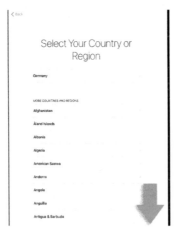

## Chapter 2: Setting up Your iPad

Now, if you have iOS 11 or 12 set up on your iPhone (or older iPad), bring your iPhone to your new iPad. You'll see a prompt on your iPhone. Tap 'continue'.

Your iPad will display a strange pattern, like the one shown below.

**Waiting for
iPhone...**

Position this image in the frame of your
other iPhone.

Use the camera on your iPhone and position the blue pattern in the circle shown on the bottom of your iPhone screen.

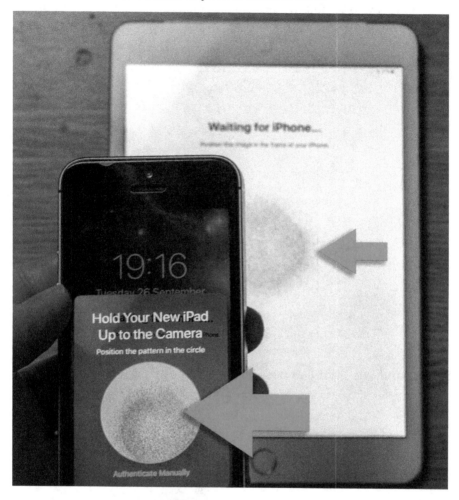

Now leave your iPhone next to your new iPad until the set up process is complete. Your new iPad will activate, you may need to enter your passcode, the same one you use to unlock your iPhone.

Follow the prompts on your iPad to set up touch ID if required

Check out the 'Auto Setup' demo in the 'using iPad' section of the video resources. Scan the code with your iPad or go to the following website.

www.elluminetpress.com/using-iPad

## Manual Setup

Turn iPad on and follow the Setup Assistant. This will guide you through the process

Swipe your finger across the bottom of the screen.

Select Language, scroll down and Select Country or Region.

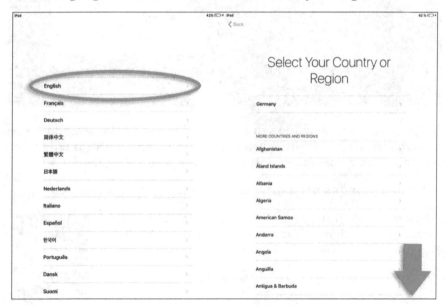

Tap 'set up manually' at the bottom of the screen.

Tap on the name of your WiFi Network. Enter your WiFi password or network key when prompted.

Tap 'Enable Location Services'. The location services allow your iPad to determine your current physical location. Some apps require this; maps and other apps that provide local information.

Enter a passcode and set up touch ID if you have it. This is used to lock your iPad and you will be prompted for this code when you open your iPad from the lock screen.

For touch ID, scan the finger you are most likely to use to press the home button with. In most cases this is your thumb, so it makes sense to scan this finger. Follow the instructions on the screen.

You'll need to scan your finger a few times, so the system can account for different variations, as you wont always put your thumb on the pad in exactly the same position every time. Do what it says on the screen. When you're done, tap 'next'.

Check out the Touch ID demo in the 'using iPad' section of the video resources on how to scan your fingerprint. Scan the code with your iPad or go to the following website.

www.elluminetpress.com/using-iPad

Tap 'set up as New iPad'. This will create a clean iPad. *If you have upgraded to a new iPad, you can tap 'restore from iCloud backup' and select the latest backup. This will set up your iPad using your previous settings and data.*

Tap sign in with your Apple ID. Enter your username and password.

Hit 'continue' to set up Siri. Follow the instructions on the screen to initialise Siri.

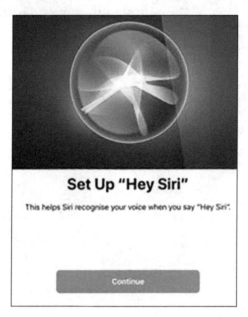

Tap "don't send" or "don't share" on 'Apple Diagnostics' and 'App Analytics'.

Tap OK to get started.

When you sign into your iPad, you will see the home screen. Lets take a closer look at the screen.

Along the top of the home screen there is a status bar that displays current networks (cellular or WiFi), current time, services such as bluetooth and battery life.

In the centre of the screen are icons representing apps that are currently installed on iPad. Some are installed already but many can be downloaded from the app store.

## Chapter 2: Setting up Your iPad

Along the bottom of the screen is the Dock. The Dock is split into two sections. On the left hand side you'll see commonly used apps: messages, web browsing, email, music, and files. You can drag and drop icons onto this part of the dock from your home screen. On the right hand side of the dock, you'll see your most recently opened apps.

At the bottom of the iPad itself, we have the home button. Whenever you want to get back to the home screen from any app, just press this button.

This diagram shows the rear. You can see volume controls and SIM card tray on the left of the diagram. On the back you'll see your camera, the headphone jack along the top and the dock connector along the bottom.

# Charging your iPad's Battery

You can plug your iPad directly into the charger to charge the battery, without having to go through a computer.

Plug the other end of the lightning cable into the port on the bottom of your iPad.

Your battery will take a few hours to charge. Best practice is not to let your battery deplete completely, charge it up when you still have about 20% charge left.

# Connecting your iPad to a Mac/PC

Your iPad lightning cable connects to the port on the bottom of your iPad.

The other end of the cable can be plugged into a PC or Mac to allow you to load on music, photos, apps etc.

# Using iTunes

To access iPad from your computer you will need to have iTunes installed. If you are using a Mac, iTunes will already be installed. If you are on a PC then you need to download the software from Apple's website.

You can download it from

www.apple.com/itunes

On iTunes' website, click the download link on the top right.

Then on the next page remove the ticks from the two boxes shown below.

### Download iTunes

X   iTunes 11.3.1 for Mac OS X

☐ Send me iTunes updates, news, and special offers.

☐ Keep me up to date with Apple news, software updates, and the latest information on products and services.

Apple Customer Privacy Policy

**Email Address**

**Location**
◉ United Kingdom
○ Other

Why do we need this?

**Download Now ⊙**

If you want apple to send you lots of notifications via email, enter email address. Otherwise leave it blank.

Click the 'download now' button. Go to your downloads folder and double click the iTunes installer. It is usually called 'iTunes6464Setup'

## Chapter 2: Setting up Your iPad

Once iTunes has installed, sign in with your Apple ID and password.

# Syncing your iPad with your Mac/PC

Plug your iPad into your computer, iTunes will take a few moments to recognise your device.

# Connecting to the Internet

With an iPad, you can connect to the internet two ways: one is using WiFi and the other is using a cellular connection if you've inserted a SIM card. In this section, we'll take a look at connecting using WiFi

## WiFi

WiFi is often faster than cellular data networks, but may not be available in many locations.

To locate nearby WiFi networks, tap Settings on your home screen.

Tap WiFi, then tap the name of the network you want to join

Enter the WiFi password or network key.

Once you have done that tap Join.

For your home WiFi, the network key or password, is usually printed on the back of your router.

The network name is sometimes called an SSID.

Use the same procedure if you are on a public hotspot such as in a cafe, library, hotel, airport and so on. You'll need to find the network key if they have one. Some are open networks and you can just connect.

When using public hotspots, keep in mind that most of them don't encrypt the data you send over the internet and aren't secure. So don't start checking your online banking account or shop online while using an unsecured connection, as anyone who is on the public WiFi hotspot can potentially gain access to anything you do.

If you're really concerned about security or use your devices on public hotspots for work, then you should consider a VPN or Virtual Private Network. A VPN encrypts all the data you send and receive over a network. There are a few good ones to choose from, some have a free option with a limited amount of data and others you pay a subscription.

Take a look at www.tunnelbear.com, windscribe.com & speedify.com

# Setting up Email Accounts

Tap the settings app icon on your home screen

Scroll down to 'accounts & passwords'.

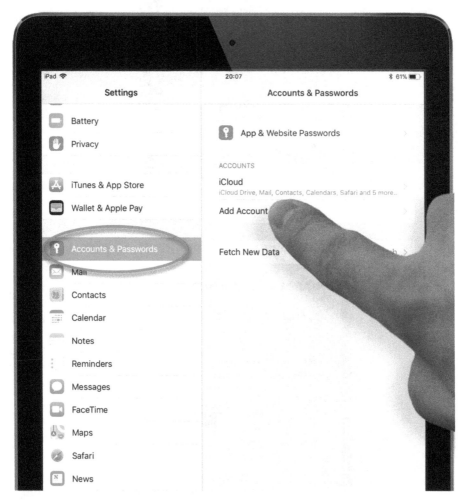

On the right hand side at the top, tap 'add account'.

Tap the type of account you want to add. If you have a Yahoo account, tap 'yahoo', if you have a Google/GMail account, tap 'google', or a Hotmail or Microsoft Account, tap 'outlook.com'.

In this example I am going to add a Microsoft Account. So I'd tap on 'outlook.com'.

In the box that appears, enter your account email address, tap 'next', then your password.

Tap 'next'.

Select 'yes' to the permission confirmation, to allow your iPad to access your email account.

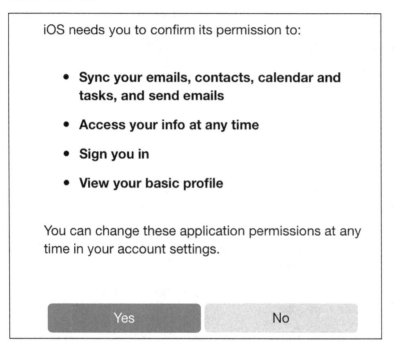

Select what you want your iPad to sync from the mail server. You can copy email, contacts, your calendar and any reminders onto your iPad by turning all the toggle switches to green, as shown below.

| Cancel | **Outlook** | Save |
|---|---|---|

Mail

Contacts

Calendars

Reminders

Tap 'Save'.

# Add Social Media Accounts

You can add your Facebook and Twitter accounts to your iPad. The easiest way to do this is to go to the App Store and download the app for Facebook, Instagram, and the app for Twitter.

Tap on the App Store icon on your home screen and in the search field on the top right type 'facebook'.

Tap 'get', next to the Facebook icon to download it. This icon might also look like a cloud if you have downloaded it before on another device, such as an iPod or iPhone.

Once it has download, hit your home button, then tap the Facebook icon on your home screen.

You can now sign in with your Facebook username and password.

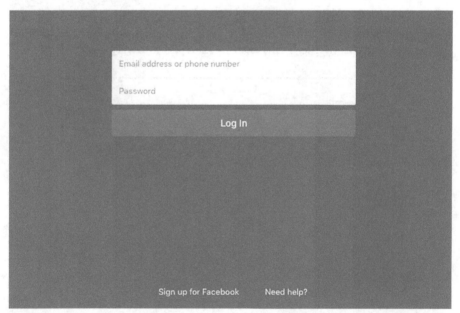

You can use the same procedure to setup Twitter, Instagram and any other social media account you have.

# Change your Wallpaper

You can set a photograph as a background on your lock screen and home screen.

You can do this from inside the Photos App. Tap the photograph you want to set.

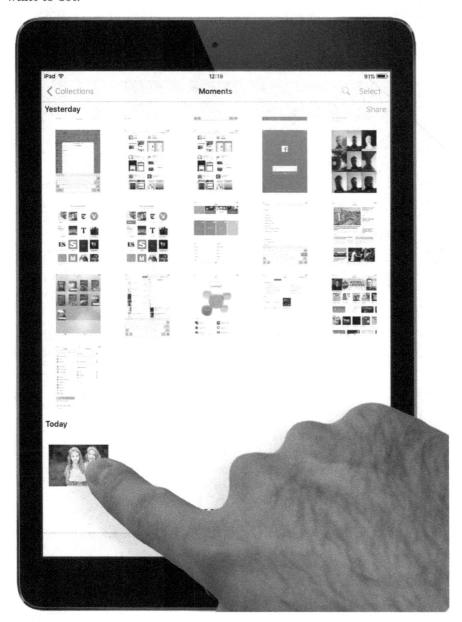

Tap the share icon on the top right of the screen. This will open up some sharing options along the bottom.

From the options that appear, select 'use as wallpaper'.

Drag the photograph with your finger until it's in the desired position. You can also make the photograph smaller, by pinching the screen with your thumb and forefinger.

To set as both home and lock screen tap 'set both'. If you just want the photo on your home screen, tap 'set home screen'. Likewise for lock screen.

# Touch ID

Open your settings app, tap Touch ID & Passcode. Enter your passcode when prompted.

Tap 'add fingerprint'.

Scan the finger you are most likely to use to press the home button with. In most cases this is your thumb, so it makes sense to scan this finger. Follow the instructions on the screen.

You'll need to scan your finger a few times, so the system can account for different variations, as you wont always put your thumb on the pad in exactly the same position every time. Do what it says on the screen. When you're done, tap 'next'.

Check out the Touch ID demo in the 'using iPad' section of the video resources on how to scan your fingerprint. Scan the code with your iPad or go to the following website

www.elluminetpress.com/using-iPad

# Face ID

Face ID is only available on the iPhone X with the TrueDepth HD camera.

Open your settings app, tap 'Face ID & Passcode'. Enter your passcode when prompted.

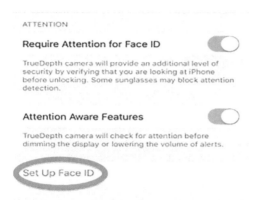

Tap 'Set Up Face ID' or 'Enrol Face' if you're setting up another ID.

Look straight at your phone then rotate your head around in a circular manner - looking left, looking up, looking right, looking down - almost like doing neck exercises, until the green marker makes it all the way around the circle. Tap 'Done' to accept.

# Chapter 3

# Getting Around Your iPad

The iPad runs Apple's own operating system called iOS. The latest version of iOS is currently version 12.

iPads have touch screens allowing you to interact with the apps on the screen using touch gestures.

Your iPad has a lot of features, we'll take a look at them in this chapter.

Lets begin by having a look at some of the iPad models on the market and the new features of iPad.

# Available Models

There are currently four models available: iPad Pro 12.9", iPad Pro 10.5", iPad 9.7", and iPad mini 4.

Lets take a look at some of the basic features of each.

## iPad Pro Series

- Comes in either 12.9" or 10.5" screen
- Three memory sizes to choose from 64GB, 256GB & 512GB
- WiFi and cellular models available
- Nano-SIM (supports Apple SIM) for cellular
- 4 speaker audio
- 12 Mega pixel camera with 4K video recording
- You can attach Apple smart keyboards and external bluetooth keyboards, useful if you use your iPad to do your work
- Works with Apple pencil - great for artists

## iPad 9.7"

- Comes in one size with 9.7" screen
- Two memory sizes available: 32GB and 128GB
- WiFi and cellular models available
- Nano-SIM (supports Apple SIM) for cellular
- 2 speaker audio
- 8 Mega pixel camera with full HD video recording
- You can even attach external bluetooth keyboards, useful if you use your iPad to do your work
- Works with Apple pencil - great for artists

## iPad Mini

- 7.9" inch screen, with 128GB memory
- Nano-SIM (supports Apple SIM) for cellular
- 2 speaker audio
- This model doesn't work with Apple pencil, so if you are an artist or like drawing etc, this might not be for you
- The iPad mini lacks a lot of features included in the iPad (9.7") and the iPad Pro series. With the iPad mini, you can't attach the smart keyboard, but you can add a bluetooth keyboard

## Choosing a Model

The best value I have found for most users is the iPad 9.7" 32GB model. 32GB of memory is enough for most, however if you like to take a lot of photos or videos and install lots of apps, then you might want to consider 128GB - the price increases sharply with more memory.

Consider what kind of connectivity to the internet you need. If you are using your iPad around the house, at work, college, library or coffee shop that has WiFi, you probably don't need the cellular option. However, if you don't have readily available access to WiFi, perhaps while travelling on a train or out and about, WiFi access might be limited or no-existent. In this case, you'd be better going for the WiFi & cellular option. Cellular internet connects in the same way as your cell phone or mobile phone. This requires a SIM card and a data plan from a phone network provider in your country.

Here's a summary of the models and prices.

| 12.9-in. iPad Pro | | | 10.5-in. iPad Pro | | | iPad | | | iPad mini 4 | | |
|---|---|---|---|---|---|---|---|---|---|---|---|
| 64GB | $799 | £769 | 64GB | $649 | £619 | 32GB | $329 | £319 | 128GB | $399 | £399 |
| 256GB | $949 | £919 | 256GB | $799 | £769 | 128GB | $429 | £409 | | | |
| 512GB | $1149 | £1119 | 512GB | $999 | £969 | | | | | | |
| Wi-Fi + Cellular | | | Wi-Fi + Cellular | | | Wi-Fi + Cellular | | | Wi-Fi + Cellular | | |
| 64GB | $929 | £899 | 64GB | $779 | £749 | 32GB | $459 | £449 | 128GB | $529 | £529 |
| 256GB | $1079 | £1049 | 256GB | $929 | £899 | 128GB | $559 | £539 | | | |
| 512GB | $1279 | £1249 | 512GB | $1129 | £1099 | | | | | | |

These features can change at any time, so for a more up to date comparison and pricing, go here:

        www.apple.com/ipad/compare/

# Sign in & Sign Out of iCloud

If you've set up your iPad from new and been through the initial setup, then your iPad will normally be signed in to your iCloud account. However if you need to sign into another iPad then you can do so from the settings app.

To **sign in**, open your settings app, tap on 'sign in to your iPad' then enter your Apple ID email address and password. Tap 'sign in'.

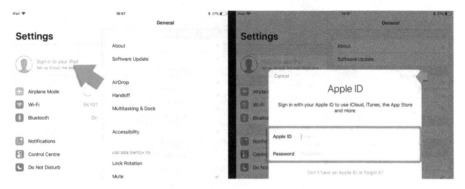

To **sign out**, open your settings app, tap on your Apple ID.

On the bottom right hand side, tap 'sign out'.

# Touch Gestures

Gestures, sometimes called multi-touch gestures, are what you'll use to interact with the touch screen on iPad.

While you work through this part, take a look at the 'navigation' section of the accompanying video resources. Scan the code or go to the following website.

www.elluminetpress.com/ipad-navigation

## Tap

Tap your index finger on an icon or to select something on the screen. For example, you can tap on an app icon, a link in safari, or even a song you want to download.

You can also tap and hold your finger on the screen to access other options that might be available (this is like right-clicking the mouse on your computer).

# Drag

Tap on the screen and without lifting your finger off the glass, slide your finger around the screen to drag up and down, left or right, and any other direction on the screen.

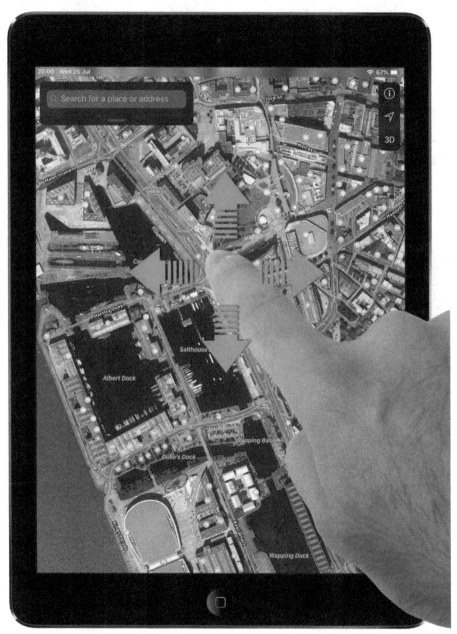

## Pinch & Spread

Hold your index finger and thumb on the area you want to zoom in or out on, then pinch the screen to zoom out and spread to zoom in.

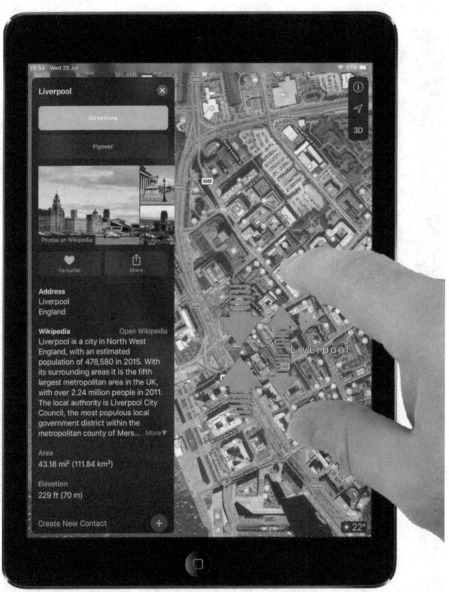

Pinch is shown in the illustration above, with the large red arrow, spread is shown with the small red arrow.

## Swipe

This allows you to flip through photos, pages in an e-book, pages on the home screen. You swipe across the screen almost like striking a match. You can swipe up, down, left, and right.

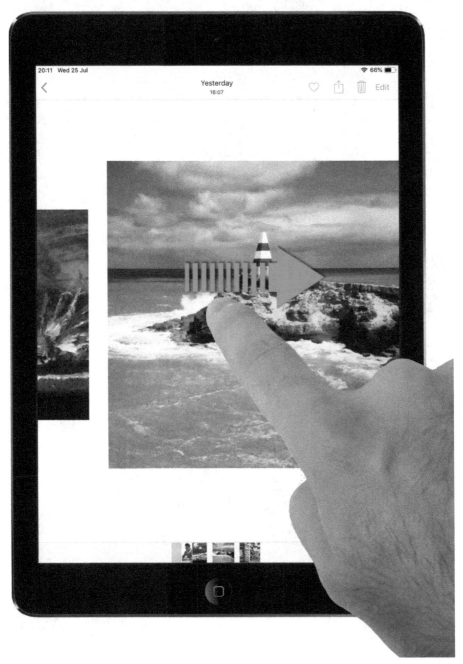

# Four Finger Swipe

Hold your four fingers (not your thumb) on the screen and swipe across to switch between open apps. You can swipe left and right.

# Home Button

While using your iPad, press the home button once to get back to your home screen, where you can select your icons to launch apps. You can also swipe upward from the bottom edge of the screen - you'll use this more if you are using an iPad X or iPhone X with no home button.

Double press your home button - that is pressing twice in quick succession - to bring up your multitasking app switcher, where you can view all your running apps, switch to a running app, or close apps.

You can also swipe upward from the bottom edge to the center of the screen, until all the app thumbnail icons appear.

## Reveal Home Screen

To reveal the home screen, press the home button once. You can also swipe upwards from the bottom of the screen - useful on an iPhone X where there is no home button.

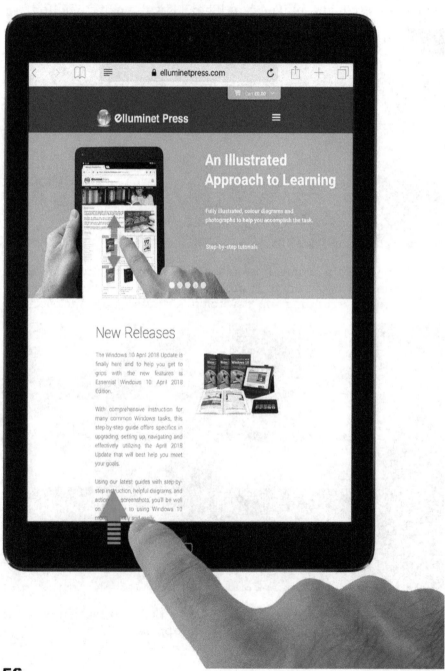

## Reveal App Switcher

To reveal the task switcher, so you can see all your running apps, press the home button twice. You can also swipe upwards from bottom edge to the center of the screen, until the app thumbnails appear - useful on an iPhone X where there is no home button.

## 3D Touch

3D touch isn't available on the iPad and is only included on the latest iPhones. Since it is part of iOS 12, it's worth taking a quick look at how it works.

We're all used to tapping on icons to start different apps or to select options and so on. 3D touch adds a new method called a press. To press on an icon means to push it, applying a bit of pressure, as if you are pressing a button.

You can now press on the icons on your home screen to quickly access some basic features, without opening the app. For example, to take a quick selfie, press on the camera icon, and from the drop down, tap 'take selfie'.

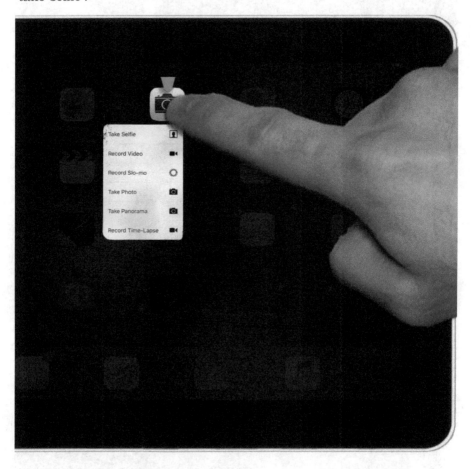

You can do this with any app on the home screen. These are called quick actions.

Another feature is called 'peek and pop'. If you are, for example, checking through your emails, you can press and hold on a message in your inbox to quickly preview the message.

A quick preview will open up. This is called 'peek'. From here, you can swipe up with your finger to reply without opening the email.

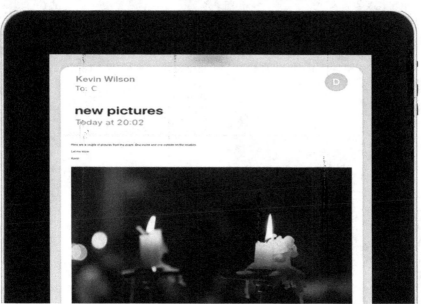

To open the email fully, press down again. This is called 'pop'. To dismiss the message, lift your finger off the screen.

You can use these features, on maps, photos, messages and so on. Give it a try and see what it does.

## Quick Peek Home Screen Icons

This particular feature only works on an iPhone and not on any of the iPads. If you tap and hold your finger on an icon either on the dock or home screen for about a second, you'll see the peek window appear. This shows you the last few items you were looking at or working on within that particular app.

For example, in the screen below, tap and hold your finger on the pages app icon - either on the dock or on the home screen.

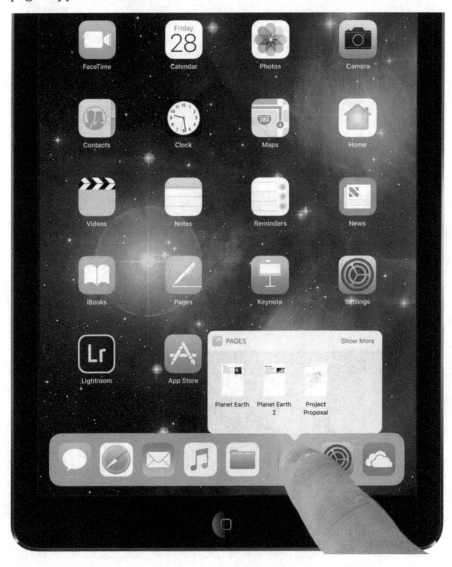

# Multitasking

iPads run an operating system called iOS. iOS is a multitasking operating system. This means that you can run more than one app at the same time. Open apps that are not currently on your screen will be running in the background. To quickly see what apps are running, press your home button twice, or swipe upwards from the bottom edge to the center of the screen, until the app thumbnail icons appear.

## Chapter 3: Getting around Your iPad

After using your iPad, you will find that there are a lot of apps running, this can severely affect the performance of your iPad and drain your battery more quickly.

To close apps, press your home button twice, then swipe your finger upwards on the app you want to close, as illustrated below.

This will close the app. Do this on all the apps you want to close.

You can also use this technique to switch between apps. Press your home button twice, then swipe your finger left and right to browse through the apps, then tap on the app you want to switch to.

Take a look at the multitasking demos in the 'using ipad' section of the accompanying video resources. Scan the code or go to the following website.

www.elluminetpress.com/using-ipad

# Open Multiple Apps at a Time

You can open multiple apps using two new methods. You can use slide over, where your app floats on top of the other and split view, where your apps run side by side.

Take a look at 'slideover feature' and 'splitscreen feature' demo of the accompanying video resources. Scan the code or go to the following website.

www.elluminetpress.com/using-ipad

## Using Slide Over

While running an app, swipe upwards from the bottom edge of the screen without lifting your finger off the glass to reveal the dock, then drag an app icon off the dock onto your screen.

Your app will open up and float on top of your screen.

You can interact with your app in the normal way and you can drag the app to either side of the screen. Use the small tab on top of the window to drag.

# Using Split View

While running an app, swipe upwards from the bottom edge of the screen without lifting your finger off the glass to reveal the dock, then drag an app icon off the dock to the edge of the screen.

Your screen will split and you'll see one app on the left hand side and the app you just opened on the right.

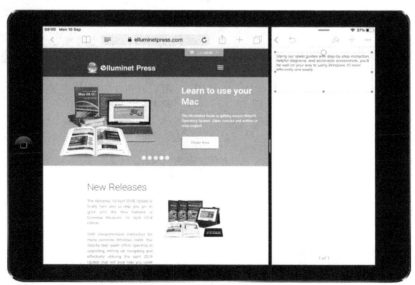

You can drag and drop information between the apps, as well as copy and paste information.

# Drag & Drop

The Drag and Drop feature allows you to drag text, photos or documents from one app to another. You can drag items within the same apps or across different apps

In the demo below, the email app is running with files app running as a slide over app, as demonstrated in the previous section.

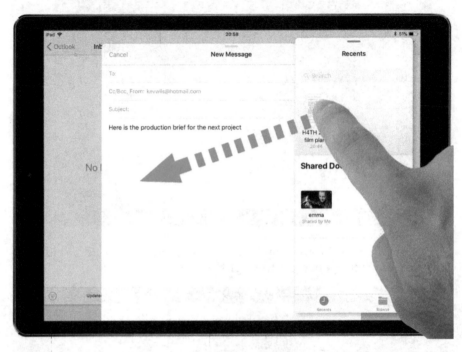

Tap and hold your finger on an item - photo or file, then drag your finger across the screen and drop the item where you want.

You can also drag and drop using the split view. Open the two apps in split view as demonstrated in the previous section.

In the demonstration above, I have the email app running in split view with the files app.

To attach the document to the email, tap and hold your finger on the document in the files app, and drag it across to the email app.

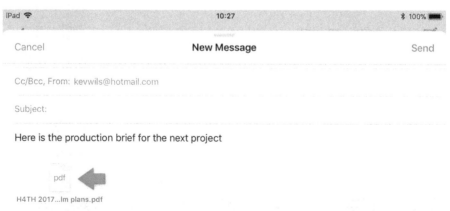

To close the slideover app, swipe the app off the edge of the screen.

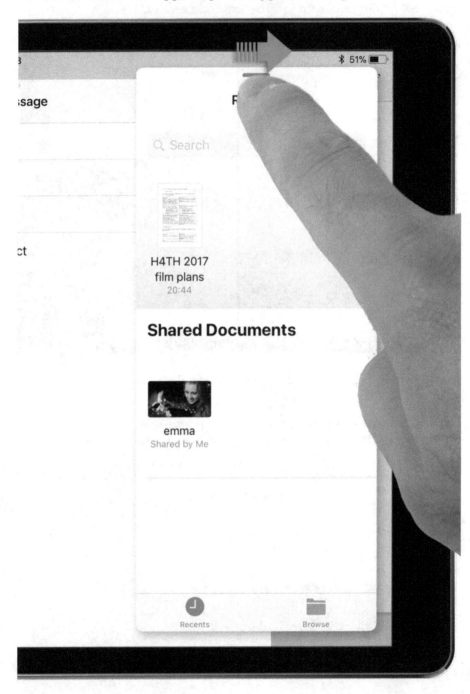

To close your splitscreen, swipe the handle on the divider off the screen.

# Control Centre

The control centre is your control hub where you can adjust screen brightness, volume, access WiFi/bluetooth controls, access your camera, and other controls.

To open control centre, swipe downwards from the top right edge of your screen.

Here you can control the volume of playing music, turn on and off WiFi, blue-tooth, access your camera, set the orientation lock to stop the screen shifting - this can be useful if you are reading a book etc.

# Customising Control Centre

To customise the controls, first open your settings app. Tap 'Control Centre' then tap 'Customise Controls'.

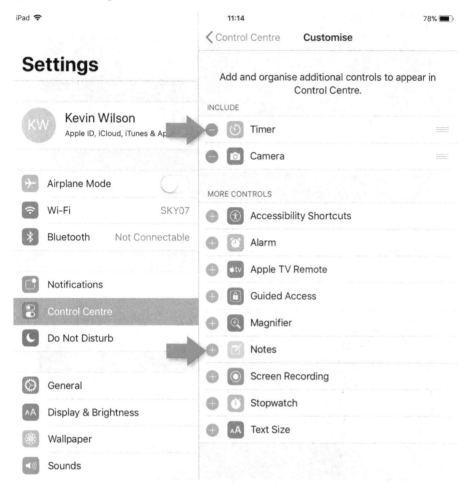

The settings for this are divided into two sections. The top section labelled 'include', shows apps and icons that will appear in the control centre. The bottom section labelled 'more controls', shows apps and features that are available but are not enabled.

To remove apps or icons from control centre, tap the red '-' next to the app name in the top section.

To add apps or icons, tap the green '+'next to the app in the bottom section. The enabled app or icon will jump to the top section, meaning it is now enabled and will show up on the control centre.

# Notifications & Lock Screen

These two have now been merged. Swipe your finger downwards from the top centre edge of the screen, to invoke the lock screen & notifications.

Notifications such as email, sms/text messages or reminders can also appear on the lock screen.

Tap on one of the notifications to see more information.

# Picture in Picture

Picture in Picture is for video. This can be FaceTime video or a film from your video library. The video shows up as a small thumbnail that can sit over the other apps you're using.

Tap the little icon on the top left of the video window while watching a video on your video player, the video will turn into a thumbnail.

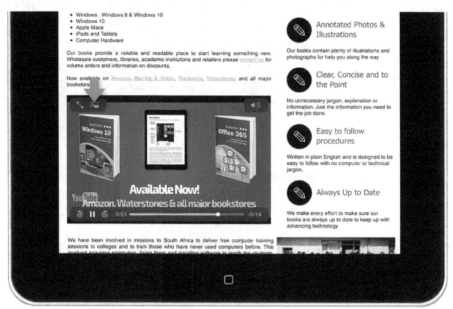

You can also drag the thumbnail into position. You can now go back to the home screen, open another app and the video will remain on top so you can see it while working on something else.

If you now go back to your home screen, the video stays in the corner

You can open any app and continue working. In this example, I am going to open the email app.

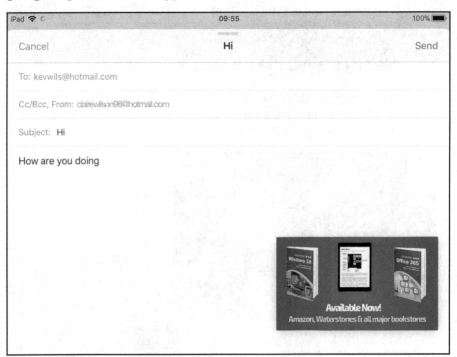

# Continuity

Continuity allows users to share documents, e-mails, and websites over WiFi to your devices.

For example, when you're working on an email, Pages document, Keynote presentation, Numbers spreadsheet, viewing a location in Maps or if you're browsing the web on your Mac, you will see on the lock screen of your iPad, the app you're currently using on your Mac.

Your iPad will allow you to pick up where you left off in that app you were using on your Mac. This is called handoff.

Tap the small icon on the bottom left of the lock screen, then swipe your finger upwards.

Continuity also allows you to reply to SMS messages and answer phone calls on you Mac and iPad. This feature is supported only by compatible Macs running Yosemite, Capitan, Sierra & Mojave or by devices running iOS 8, 9, 10, 11 & 12.

# The On-screen Keyboard

Typing on an iPad is easy, using the on-screen Multi-Touch keyboard. Tap in any text field, email, document or message, and the on screen keyboard will pop up on the bottom of the screen.

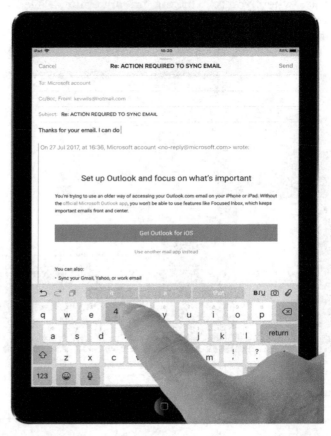

You can tap on the keys to type. To access the numbers and symbols on the top half of the key, tap and slide your finger down on the key. This is like holding down the shift key on a computer. For example, to type 4, tap and slide your finger down on the letter R.

Lets take a closer look at the keyboard. You'll notice some icons and information along the top of they keyboard. Some of these will depend on which app you are typing in but most have a similar function.

Here is an example from the email app.

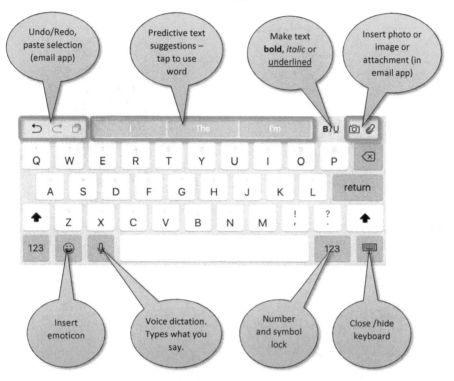

Along the top you will see some predictive text suggestions that appear according to what you're typing in. If the correct word appears, you can quickly tap on the appropriate suggestion instead of typing in the whole word.

On either side of the predictive text section, you'll see some app specific icons. These are usually shortcuts to common tools used in these apps. For example inserting photos or attachments in our email example or changing text to bold or italic.

Some icons along the bottom worth noting are: the '123' key, this locks in numbers and symbols so you can quickly enter a series of numbers just by tapping the keys. The 'smiley face' icon, these are emojis or emoticons - small smiley faces, thumbs up, expressions, and small images that are intended to show how you're feeling in your messages; happy, angry, amused and so on. Finally the 'microphone icon', this is a dictation tool that transcribes or types out voice dictations.

# Apple Smart Keyboard

If you have an iPad pro, you can use the Apple Smart Keyboard, however there are third party bluetooth keyboards that will work on the iPad mini and iPad 9.7".

On the iPad pro, the iPad keyboard slots into a special connector on the side.

iPad Pro 12.9" or 10.5" Model

Apple Smart Keyboard with dock connector

# Bluetooth Keyboards

If you are using the iPad 9.7" or the iPad mini you'll need to use a bluetooth keyboard. You can pick them up online or at any computer store.

To pair a bluetooth keyboard with your iPad, you'll need to put the keyboard into 'pairing mode' - see the instructions that came with your keyboard to find out how to do this.

Once your keyboard is in 'pairing mode', open the settings app on your iPad and tap 'bluetooth'. Turn bluetooth on if it isn't already.

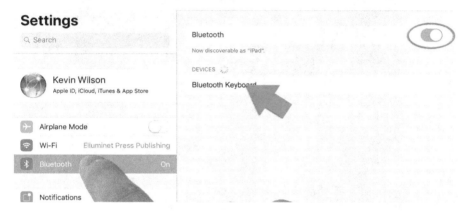

Tap the "Wireless Keyboard" device in the list of discovered bluetooth devices. You may need to wait a minute if it doesn't show right away.

On the keyboard, enter the 4-digit code that pops up on your iPad screen.

Once your keyboard has been connected or paired, you can type normally instead of using the onscreen keyboard.

This is useful if you are using Apple Pages to create a word processed document or typing an email, as the physical keyboard is much easier to use than the onscreen keyboard.

# Spotlight Search

Spotlight is integrated with a number of web services so that users can search using Wikipedia, Bing, or Google. Other services include: news, nearby places, suggested websites, movie show times, and content that is not already on the device from the iTunes Store

You can activate spotlight search by swiping your finger downwards from the centre of your home screen.

Once you have spotlight's search screen, you can type your search into the search field at the top of the screen.

Search also gives you some suggestions. These are listed below the search field and are the most commonly searched for entries for your search term. In the example below, I am searching for anything relating to 'computer'. Tap on the entry that best matches your search, or press enter on your on screen keyboard.

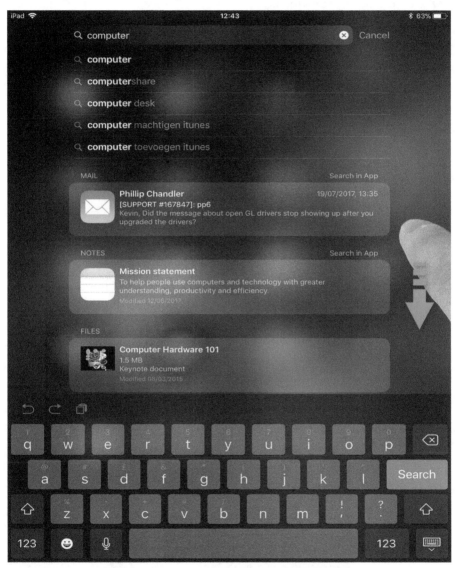

Scroll down the list to see files, apps, websites, news articles, and suggested websites according to your search terms.

Tap on one of the items to open it up.

You can track flights. This is a useful feature, especially if you have arranged to pick up a friend or collect a colleague from the airport.

If you have the flight number, enter it into spotlight search. There might be more than one flight, so make sure you confirm the correct departure and arrival times.

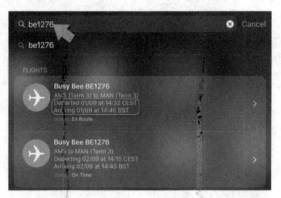

Tap on the flight to view tracking details. Here you'll see the current position of the aircraft on the map, which terminal the plane is arriving at and what time it is arriving - this plane is arriving at terminal 3 at 14:45.

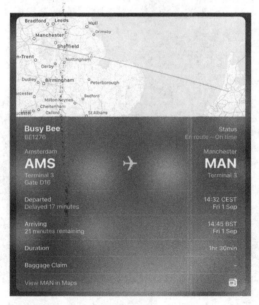

Underneath you'll also see baggage claim timings and how long passengers are expected to get through. At the bottom you can find driving directions to the airport using the maps app.

# Arranging Icons

To move an icon, tap and hold your finger on the icon, then drag your finger across the screen.

The other icons on the screen will automatically move and rearrange themselves around the icon you're moving.

To move the icon onto another page, drag the icon to the right or left edge of the screen. Once the icon page turns, release your finger.

You can get to the other pages by swiping your finger left and right to turn the page

The two little dots, circled in the illustration above, show you what page you are on and how many pages of icons you have. This will vary depending on what apps you have installed. In this example, there are two pages.

You can identify what page you are on by looking at this icon, the one in bold is the page you are on. In this example, page 1.

Take a look at the 'arranging icons' video demo of the accompanying video resources. Scan the code or go to the following website.

www.elluminetpress.com/ipad-navigation

# Removing Icons

This effectively deletes the app from your iPad. To do this, tap and hold your finger on the app's icon you want to delete, until you see a small x appear on the top left of the icons.

Tap on the x on the top left of the icon to delete it.

If you want to delete any other apps, tap the x on the icons. Press the home button when you're finished.

# Adding Icons to the Dock

You can also add your most used apps to the dock at the bottom of the screen.

To do this, tap, and drag the icon to the dock.

# Siri

Siri is an extremely useful feature. She allows you to talk to your iPad, sometimes referred to as a virtual assistant; she can help you with all kinds of things. You can use Siri to send messages, schedule meetings, and search for nearby restaurants all without having to type a single letter.

## Using Siri

To use Siri, press and hold the Home button on your device until she appears. Then tell her what you need.

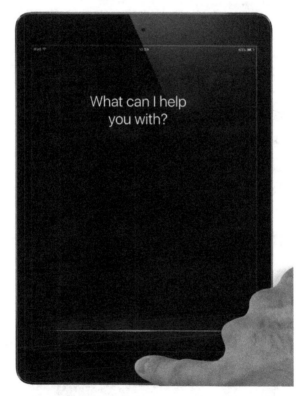

Try some of the following phrases...

*Try saying: "Hey Siri"*
*Try saying: "Send email to..." (pick a name from your contacts list)*
*Try saying: "What is the weather like tomorrow"*
*Try saying: "Find me a website on baking a cake"*
*Try saying: "Remind me to pick up milk on the way home"*
*Try saying: "Call..." (pick a name from your contacts list).*

## Siri Translate

Here's a good one for those who love to travel but don't speak the local language. At the time of writing, Siri can only translate from US English to French, German, Italian, Mandarin and Spanish.

If you're using Siri with any language other than US English, you'll need to change this in the settings app. Tap 'Siri & Search', tap to change the language to 'English (United States)', circled below.

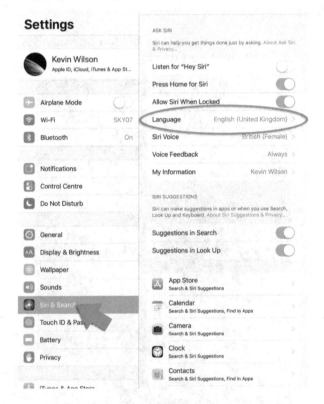

To use the translator, hold down the home button until Siri appears and speak the word **"Translate"**.

Siri will ask you which language you want to translate into. Say the language name or tap the option from the list. In this demonstration, I'm going to use Spanish.

Now speak the phrase you want to translate into the language you just selected.

To play the translation again, tap the play button next to the translation.

You can also say "How do I say <u>where is the train station</u> in <u>spanish</u>?"

Just replace the underlined bits of the phrase for the phrase and language you want to translate into.

# Voice Dictation

Another useful feature of Siri is voice dictation, which allows you to enter text without having to use the keyboard. You can search the web, take notes, post an update to Facebook, and more just by speaking.

To use voice dictation, tap the microphone icon on your on screen keyboard.

*If the icon isn't there go to your settings app, tap 'general', then 'keyboard'. Go down to 'enable dictation' and switch the slider to on.*

Then start dictating the text you want Siri to type. She listens to what you say, and types it. The more you use it, the better Siri gets at understanding you.

You can even add punctuation by saying words like "period" or 2 "question mark" when you reach the end of a sentence. Tap the keyboard icon on the bottom right to close dictation mode.

# Settings Search

Tap on the settings app. On the main screen at the top left, swipe your finger down under the word 'settings'

This will reveal the settings search field.

In the search field, type in the setting you want to change. I'm adding my email accounts so I'll type 'mail' in this example.

Tap on 'mail' in the search results.

**91**

# Family Sharing

You can now add six others users as family members. You can share iTunes and Apps, Apple Music, iCloud Storage, your location and authorize your kid's spending on the app store.

To set this up, go to settings and select your ID. Tap 'Set Up Family Sharing'. Then tap 'get started'.

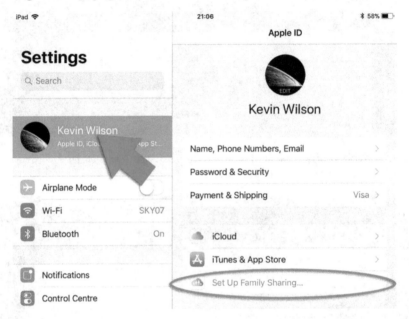

You'll see a screen with four options. You can share any of these options later on but this screen is asking which one you want to begin with. If you want to share books, apps, films and music; select the first option.

Tap 'continue' to confirm you want to use your Apple ID to share your purchases.

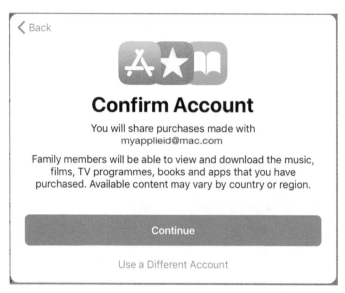

Confirm the payment details you want to share. Any member of your family that requests an app will be charged to this payment method on your approval. If you want to use another one tap 'use different payment method' and enter the card details.

Tap 'continue' if you want to use your default Apple ID payment method.

Tap 'invite family members'. Select 'invite in person' and enter their Apple ID email address. If they don't have an email address or too young, tap 'create a child account'.

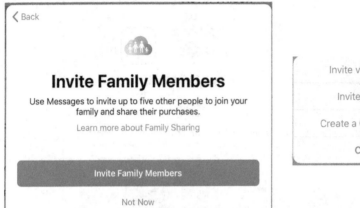

## Add a Family Member

Go to settings, select your ID. Tap 'family sharing then tap 'add family member'.

Now select how you want to invite them. You can invite then 'in person', ie enter their Apple ID email address, send an invitation via iMessage or 'create a new child account'.

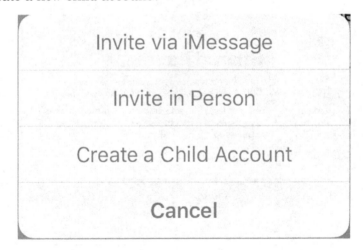

# Invite in Person

Select 'invite in person' from the popup. Enter the person's Apple ID email address and password. If their details are in your address book, you'll see a suggestion underneath. Tap on the name if it's correct.

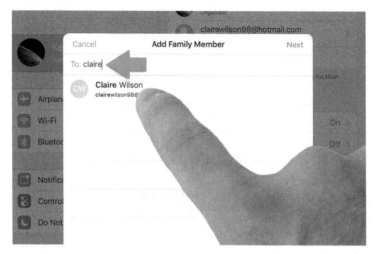

When the person signs into their iPad and checks their email, they'll see an invitation to join the family.

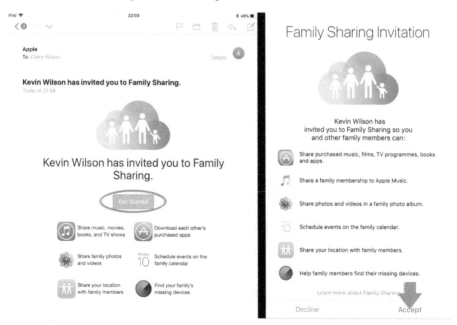

Click 'get started', then click 'accept' on the confirmation.

## Child Accounts

If you have young children it makes sense to create separate accounts for them rather than allowing them to use yours. This helps to protect them and to help you monitor what your child is up to.

To create a child account, go to settings, select your ID. Tap 'family sharing' then tap 'add family member'. From the popup select 'create child account'.

Now follow the instructions on screen. Tap 'next' on the top right of the screen.

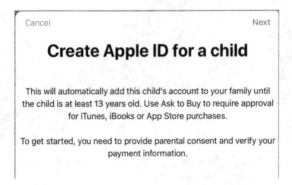

Enter your child's birthday using the rollers on the bottom of the screen, then tap next.

Agree to the disclosure, tap 'agree'.

Enter your CVV code from the credit card you have registered with your Apple ID. Tap 'next'.

Enter your child's first and last name using the on-screen keyboard, then tap 'next'.

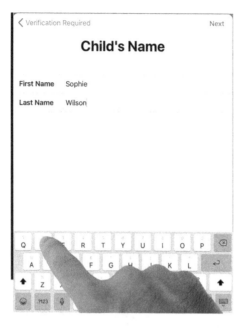

Enter an Apple ID email them. Tap 'next'.

Enter a password for them and tap 'next'.

This will create a new account for your child to use.

Now, select some security questions that you will remember the answers to. This is a security step that will be used to identify you when you need to change a password or recover a forgotten password.

Select a question from the 'question' field and type in an answer in the 'answer' field. Tap 'agree' to accept the terms and conditions

Enable 'ask to buy'. This means that if your child tries to buy an app from the app store, a music track, tv show or film, you will receive an authorisation request where you can approve the purchase or deny it. Tap 'next'.

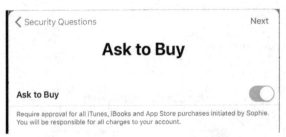

Now allow your child to sign into their iPad with the Apple ID email address and password you just created. In this example it would be sophie20077@icloud.com

# Managing your Family

Family members can share purchased apps, music, and books using the same credit card. iPad can also automatically set up photo streams for all family members. Calendars may be synced between all members.

Kids can also send iTunes and App Store download requests for apps, music, movies, and more to their parents provided this service is set up correctly.

On your device, tap 'review' from the prompt to see details of the request.

# Screen Time

Screen Time collects usage statistics on the various apps you use on your iPad. It records how much time you've spent using a particular app, can generate activity reports, allows you to set app time limits, and can be useful for monitoring your kid's activity.

You can find screen time on your settings app. On the left hand side of the settings app, select 'screen time'.

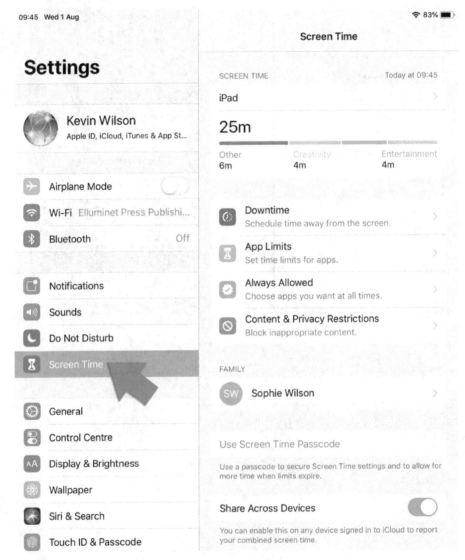

Lets take a look at the main screen.

SCREEN TIME                    Today at 09:45

iPad                                              >

## 25m

| Other | Creativity | Entertainment |
| 6m | 4m | 4m |

Breakdown of usage stats of apps used on your iPad

Set a period of time when your apps will be unavailable

**Downtime**
Schedule time away from the screen.                >

**App Limits**
Set time limits for apps.                          >

**Always Allowed**
Choose apps you want at all times.                 >

**Content & Privacy Restrictions**
Block inappropriate content.                       >

FAMILY

SW   Sophie Wilson                                 >

Use Screen Time Passcode

Use a passcode to secure Screen Time settings and to allow for
more time when limits expire.

**Share Across Devices**

You can enable this on any device signed in to iCloud to report
your combined screen time.

Turn Off Screen Time

Add time limits to specific genres of apps. Eg 1 hour for games

Add apps that are allowed to run regardless of set limits

Allow or block certain content or apps. Eg age appropriate films

Set a passcode to prevent users from changing screen time restrictions

## Downtime

With downtime, you can set a period of time, say a couple of hours, that your iPad apps are unavailable.

Select 'downtime' from the main screen, and turn it on using the switch at the top.

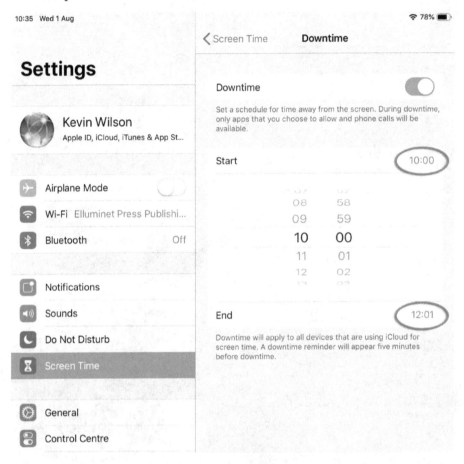

Below, you'll see two options appear. Use this to set the start and end times you want apps to be unavailable. Tap on the times to change them.

For example, you could set it from 9pm to 7am. This would mean, from 9pm, your iPad apps will turn off until 7am the next morning - preventing you from using your iPad late at night.

You could also set a limit so if your children use the iPad, they can't use it until a certain time - perhaps after they've done their homework.

# App Limits

You can set the length of time you want a particular app to be available. To do this, select 'app limits' from the main screen, then tap 'add limit'.

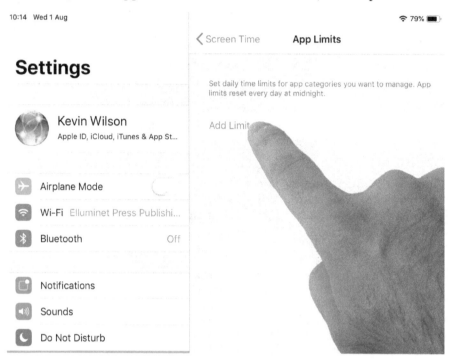

Choose the genre of apps you want to add the limit to. In this example I'm adding a limit to all social networking apps such as facebook, instagram and so on, then tap 'add'.

Set the length of time using the sliders indicated with the red arrow.

Time                                           1 hr,

                                    28
                          0         29
                    1 hour    30
                          2         3
                          3         32

Customise Days

If you want different times on different days, select 'customise days'. This will allow you to input different time limits on different days. Eg, you might want to allow more time at the weekends. Tap on the time limits to change them.

⏶ 76% 🔋

❮ Back        **Customise Days**

Sunday                                5 h
Monday                                3 hrs
Tuesday                               3 hrs, 2
Wednesday                             3 hrs, 2 min
Thursday                              3 hrs, 2 min
Friday                                3 hrs, 2 min
Saturday                              5 hrs, 2 min

Tap 'back' to return to the previous screen.

❮ App Limits    **Social Networking**

Time                              1 hr, 30 min

                          28

Tap the set time on the top right to confirm.

# Always Allowed

This allows you to choose the apps you want to be available regardless of any content restrictions or time restrictions that are set. Tap the green + to add an app from the list, or tap the red - to remove an app.

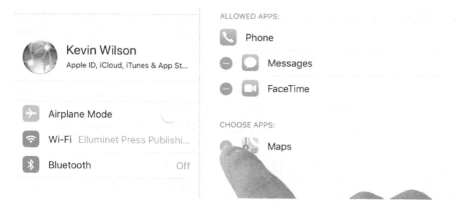

# Content & Privacy Restrictions

Content & Privacy allows you to set restrictions on certain content such as age appropriate films and television programs, or songs, websites, and books with adult themes. This is useful if your kids are using the iPad.

To set content & privacy restrictions, from the settings app, on the screen time page, select 'content & privacy restrictions'.

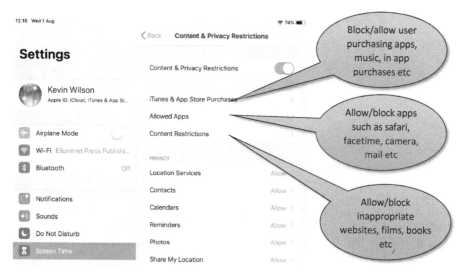

## Allowing and Blocking Content

Go to the 'content & privacy restrictions' section of screen time. From here you can add restrictions on content, apps and websites.

Tap the options to make your selections about what content to allow and what content to block.

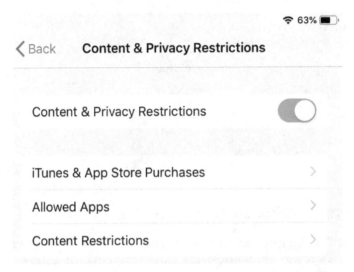

For example, to allow or block app store purchases, tap 'iTunes & App Store Purchases'

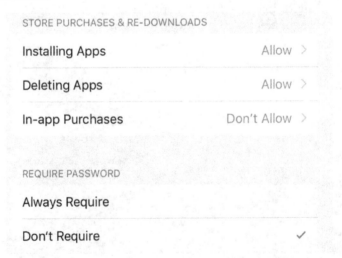

Change the setting to 'allow' to allow the feature, change it to 'don't allow' to deny the feature.

You can do the same for content restrictions such as age appropriate apps, films and websites.

To change these settings, tap 'content restrictions'

ALLOWED STORE CONTENT

| | |
|---|---|
| Ratings For | United Kingdom > |
| Music, Podcasts & News | Clean > |
| Music Profiles & Posts | On > |
| Films | PG > |
| TV Programmes | Allow All TV Programmes > |
| Books | Clean > |
| Apps | 12+ > |

WEB CONTENT

| | |
|---|---|
| Web Content | Limit Adult Websites > |

SIRI

| | |
|---|---|
| Web Search Content | Allow > |
| Explicit Language | Don't Allow > |

Tap on and change the settings appropriately. For example, to only allow PG rated films, tap 'films' and select 'PG'

Do the same for websites, web search content and language. Tap and set these to the appropriate settings, as shown in the example above.

# Chapter 4

# Internet, Email, Communication

Your iPad has a lot of features that allow you to connect to the internet, browse the web, send and receive emails, share pictures with friends, store addresses and contacts, have video chat conversations with friends and family.

To do this, Apple have provided some built in apps; Safari for web browsing, Mail for email and Face Time for video chat.

You also have apps for social media, and an address book to keep track of contacts addresses and details.

Lets start by taking a look at Safari web browser.

# Using Safari

To launch safari, tap on the safari icon located on your dock.

This will launch safari. Lets take a look at the main screen.

In safari's main screen, tap in the website address field, to enter the website's address, or Google search keyword.

Two menus to take note of. The first menu is on the left hand side of the screen and allows you to access favourite or bookmarked sites. You can tap on any of these in the list to return to the sites.

The second, is on the right hand side and allows you to share the current website link via text message, email or social media. Just tap on the icon to share the site on twitter or facebook, email the link or send it via text.

Along the bottom of that menu, you can add the current site to bookmarks/favourites. To do this tap bookmark.

Hit the + sign to add a new tab where you can open another website, Google search, favourite and so on.

The final icon on the right hand side, allows you to see all the tabs you currently have open

Safari will display your open tabs/websites as thumbnail previews, you can tap on to open up.

# Reader View

Reader view makes it easier to read web pages without all the unnecessary background clutter that usually comes with a website.

Reader view is not available on all web pages but is on most. To enable reader view, tap the reader icon on the left hand side of the web address search field.

Here you can see on the left, the normal view and on the right you can see the reader view.

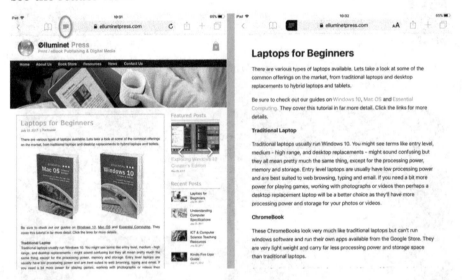

The reader view is designed to improve readability on screen and often removes a lot of graphics, photos and other media, so it's worth keeping this in mind if you are visiting media rich websites.

Tap the same icon to go back to normal view.

Check out the safari demos in the 'internet & email' section of the accompanying resources. Scan code or go to following website.

www.elluminetpress.com/ipad-comms

# Using Email

To start the mail app, tap Mail on the bottom of the screen.

Once your email is setup it will open on the main screen. The email app works best if you use your iPad in horizontal orientation. On the left hand side, is a list of all your emails. Just tap on one to view.

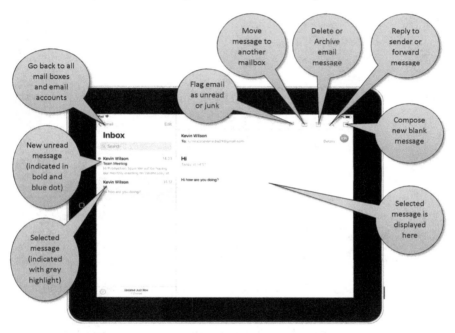

To reply to an email, select the email you want from your inbox, then tap the 'reply to sender' icon on the top right.

To forward or print an email, tap and hold your finger on the 'reply to sender' icon, and select 'forward' to forward the email to someone else. Tap 'print' to print the email.

**113**

To send a new message, click the 'compose new email' icon on the top right. This will bring up a new email. Tap in the 'To:' field to enter an email address. If you are replying to a message, the email address of the person that sent you the message will appear here automatically.

Tap in the subject field and add some text.

Tap in the message body underneath and type your message using the pop up on screen keyboard.

If you look on the top of the on screen keyboard you'll see some icons.

On the left, you can undo/redo text - undo is a good one if you make a mistake with your typing. You can also paste some text or an image you have copied from somewhere else. In the centre you have some text predictions - this shows up words you're most likely to type while writing your email - tap word to insert into message. Over on the right, you can change your text to bold, italic or underlined. You can insert a photo directly from your camera, and add an attachment.

When you have finished, tap 'send'.

To save time, if you have 3D touch enabled, you can press and hold on a message in your inbox to quickly preview the message.

A quick preview will open up. This is called 'peek'. From here, you can swipe up with your finger to reply without opening the email.

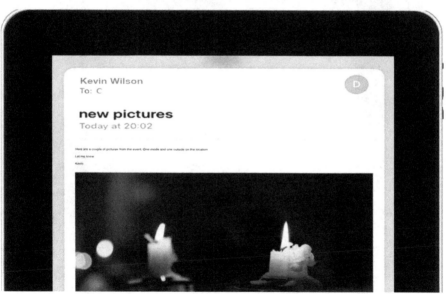

To open the email fully, press down again. This is called 'pop'. To dismiss the message, lift your finger off.

Check out the email demos in the 'internet & email' section of the accompanying resources. Scan code or go to following website.

www.elluminetpress.com/ipad-comms

# Contacts

The Contacts App is your address book. It contains all the names, email addresses, phone numbers and addresses of the people you correspond with.

Launch address book by tapping on the icon on your home screen.

This is the main screen. You can browse contacts, or add new ones.

Tap on the + sign to add a new contact.

On the screen that appears, enter the person's name and contact details in the fields.

Add their phone number, and email addresses in the relevant fields.

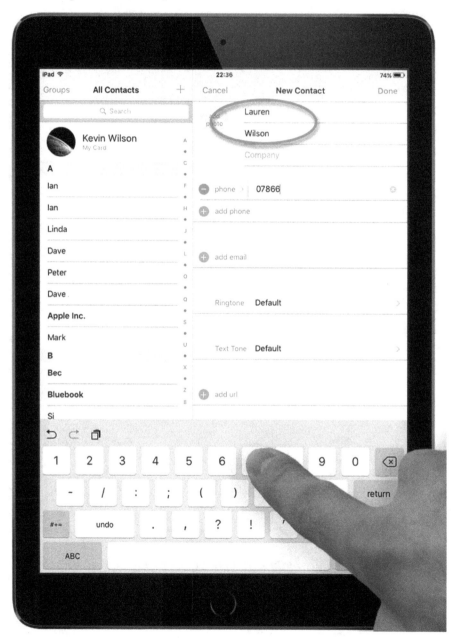

Tap 'done'.

You can also add a contact from an email message. Open the email message in the Mail App and tap on their name at the top of the email.

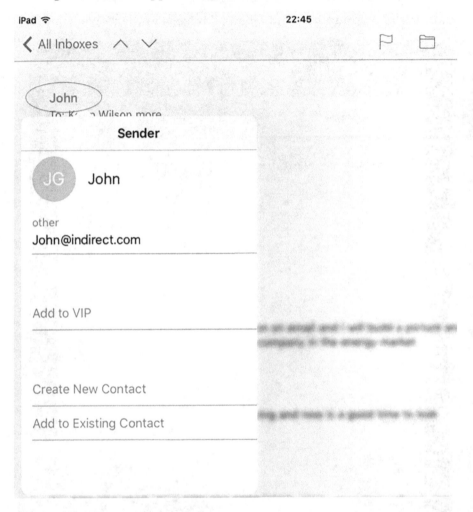

Tap 'create new contact'. iPad will automatically add the names and email address the message was sent from.

Tap done.

*You can do the same with text messages in iMessage. Tap on the message, then tap 'details', tap the 'i' icon (top right), tap 'create new contact'. Enter their name and details in the screen that appears.*

To view a contact's details, tap on the name. From here you can send a message, FaceTime them if they have it or give them a call.

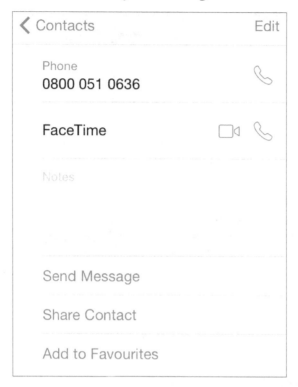

Tap 'edit' to amend any of their details.

Check out 'adding contacts' and 'contacts from email message' demos in the 'internet & email' section of the video resources.

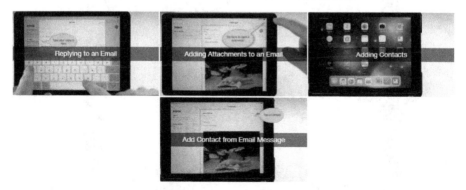

Scan the code with your iPad or go to the following website.

www.elluminetpress.com/ipad-comms

# Calendar (iCal)

To start calendar app, tap the icon on the main screen

This will bring up the calendar main screen. I found it easiest to view the calendar in month or week view. Below is in month view.

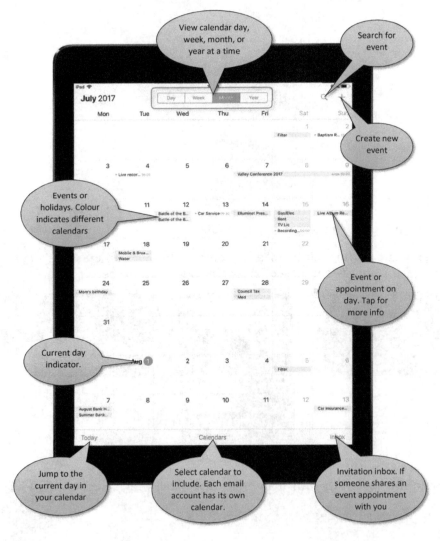

# Adding an Appointment

To add an event to the calendar, tap and hold your finger on the day the event falls on.

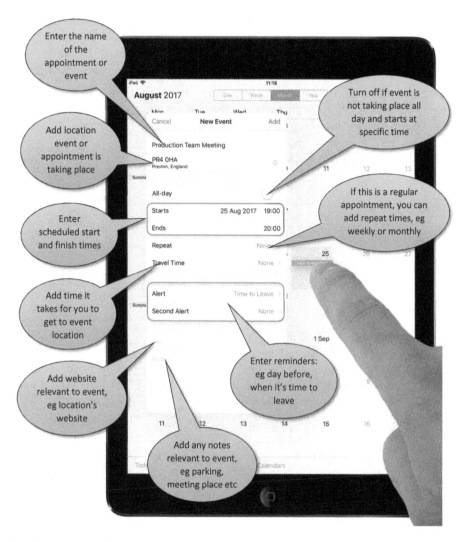

In the popup that appears. Tap 'title', then type a title (what the event or appointment is).

Do the same for location, and select your times.

Once you are finished tap done.

## Add a Recurring Appointment

To add a recurring event to the calendar, tap and hold your finger on the first day the event falls on.

In the popup that appears. Tap 'title', then type a title (what the event or appointment is).

Do the same for location, and select your times.

Now to create a recurring event, tap 'repeat' in the 'new event' window. Here you can set the event to recur once a week, once a month, every two weeks and so on. All you have to do is tap on the one you want.

You can also set a custom option, tap 'custom'. Say the event occurs every three weeks. Set the frequency to 'weekly'. Then tap 'every' and select the number of weeks. In this example, three weeks, so slide the number to '3'.

| Frequency | Weekly |
|---|---|
| Every | 3 weeks |

|  |  |
|---|---|
| 1 | |
| 2 | |
| 3 | weeks |
| 4 | |
| 5 | |

Once you are finished, tap 'repeat' on the top left of the repeat window to go back. Tap 'add' to add the event to your calendar.

# Adding an Appointment from a Message

Apple Mail, iMessage and FaceTime will scan your message for phrases that look like dates and times and will create a link in the email for you. To add the event from the email or text message, tap on this link. From the popup box tap 'create event'.

Enter a title and location if calendar didn't pick one up from the email. You can also tweak the information and add additional information if required.

Once you have done that, tap 'add' to enter the appointment into your calendar.

# FaceTime

To use FaceTime, tap the icon on the home screen. You will need your Apple ID and a wifi/data connection to the internet.

When you open FaceTime, you will be prompted to sign in if you haven't already done so.

Once FaceTime has opened, you'll see in the main window a preview of your camera. On the left hand side you'll see a darkened panel where you'll find your contacts, history of calls and a search for you to search for people

# Making a Call

In this demonstration, Claire is going to FaceTime Sophie from her iPad. Start typing the person's name you want to FaceTime into the search field on the top left of the screen. If the name is in your contacts, then it will appear underneath. Tap the little camera icon next to the name to make a FaceTime call.

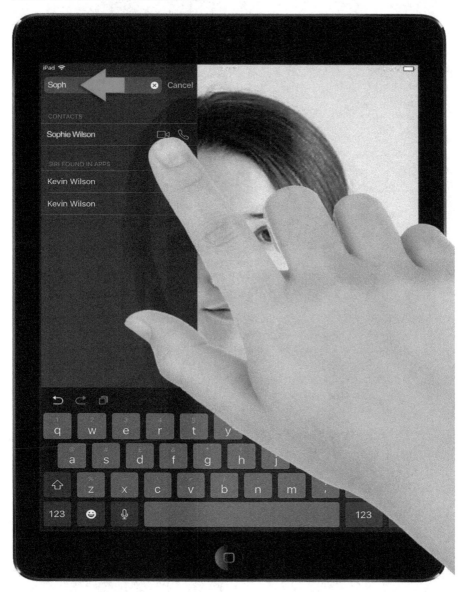

Wait for the other person to answer...

Claire's iPad is on the left in the demo below. She is placing a FaceTime call to Sophie who's using the iPad on the right.

You can see on Sophie's iPad on the right, it's telling her who is calling with the caller id at the top of the screen.

In the background of your screen, you'll see a preview of your camera - so make sure you're squarely in the frame so when the call is answered, the other person can see you clearly.

Along the bottom of the screen you'll see some icons. The red 'decline' button, declines the call. To answer the call just tap the green 'accept' button.

You'll also see two other icons above these two. Tap 'remind me' to set a reminder to call back. If you can't talk, tap 'message' to send a quick message such as 'on my way', 'can I call you later', or 'cant talk now'.

Once the other person answers, you can now have a video conversation. The onboard microphone on your iPhone/iPad will pick up your voice, so just talk naturally.

You'll see an image of the person calling in the centre of your screen with a thumbnail view of your own camera on the top right. Here's the view of Claire's call from her iPad.

Along the bottom, you'll see three icons. If these icons disappear, tap the screen once and they'll re-appear. The icon on the left opens up your effects panel, the middle icon closes the call, and the right hand icon opens up the panel fully.

It's a great tool to keep in touch with family, see the kids if you're away, and so they can see you too.

During your call, tap on the screen to reveal the in call icons

Tap on the three dots icon on the right to reveal the full panel.

On the top row of icons you have a button for adding effects, ending the call, and switching between front and rear camera on your iPad.

On the second row you have buttons to mute your microphone, mute iPad speaker, and blank your camera.

Under these icons you can open an iMessage conversation and see contact details of the person you're face-timing with.

# Adding Effects

During a call, you can add all sorts of effects to your image. To do this, tap the effects icon on the bottom left of the in call window.

Select the type of effect you want to add. You can add filters, text, shapes, and icons. In this example we're going to add a text effect.

Tap the text icon, select an effect,

Then type in some text and drag the effect into place.

Lets have a look at what the effect will look like. This is what the other person you're talking to will see.

Tap the small x on the top right of the effects panel to close. Tap the effects icon to close the panel.

Try some of the other effects and filters on the panel. Try adding a shape or an icon and see what happens.

## Group FaceTime

Group FaceTime allows you to set up groups and chat to up to 32 people at a time. To use Group FaceTime, all participants must have iOS 12 installed, otherwise you won't be able to add them to the group.

To place a group call, on the left hand panel tap on the + icon on the upper corner.

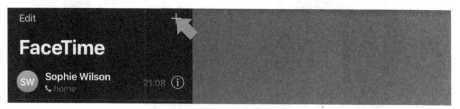

Type the names of the people you want to place a group call to in the 'to' field, or tap the + icon and add them from your contacts list.

If they all have iOS 12 installed on their devices, you'll see two green buttons appear along the bottom of the side panel.

Tap on 'video' to place a group video call.

When your contacts answer, you'll see a thumbnail of each of them on your main display.

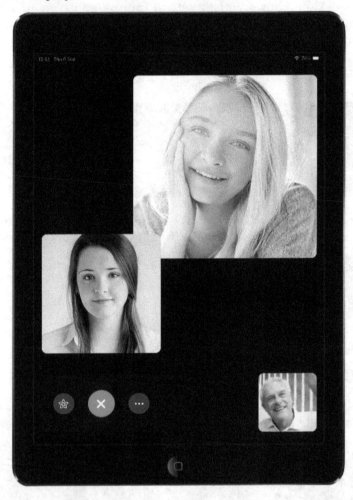

In this demo, the girls are having a group FaceTime with grand dad.

You'll see a thumbnail of your own camera in the bottom right of the screen. The other contacts in your group will show up in a thumbnail window in the main area of the screen.

The clever bit is, when one of your contacts starts talking, their thumbnail window will temporarily enlarge. As usual, Sophie is doing all the talking so her thumbnail window is enlarged.

FaceTime is useful for keeping in touch with family and friends who don't live near by, or live in another country.

## Adding a Contact

To add a contact, type the person's email address into the search field on the left hand side of the screen and tap on the email address that pops up below.

From the selections tap 'add new contact'. This will allow you to enter their name, address, phone numbers and so on.

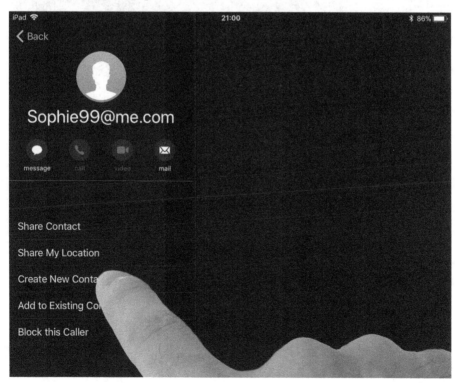

Enter the person's details into the correct fields.

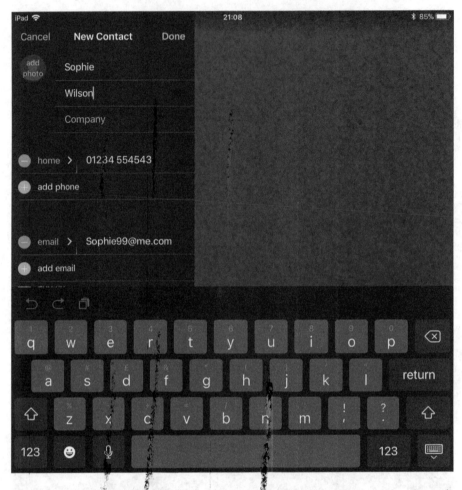

Tap in each field and add the information using the onscreen keyboard. You don't have to fill in every field, just the ones that are relevant.

Tap on 'add photo' on the top left. You can either take a photo using your camera, or select one from your photo library.

Tap 'done' when you're finished.

# iMessage

You can send photos and videos and also voice messages to anyone with an Apple device. To start iMessage, tap the icon on the dock on your home screen.

When you open iMessage, you will see a list of all your received messages. Tap on a message to read and reply. Tap the new message icon on the top of the messages list on the left hand pane.

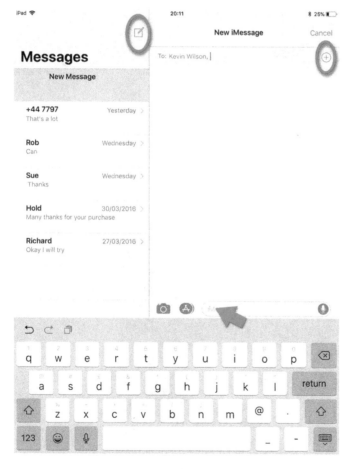

Tap the + sign to add an address or phone number from your contacts.

Type your message in the box indicated with the red arrow.

You can send a voice message by tapping and holding your finger on the mic icon. Record your message, then release your finger to stop.

From the options that appear, select from the icons below.

To send a photograph or video, tap the small camera icon on the bottom left of your message window.

Your camera app will open up. Select 'photo' from the list on the bottom right, then tap on the white circle to take the picture.

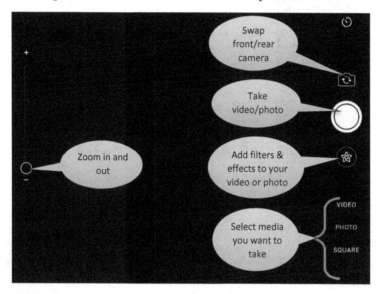

Once you've taken your photo, you can add effects and annotate the image before you send it. Just tap the markup icon on the right hand side of the screen. Tap 'save' on the top right, then tap the blue arrow to send.

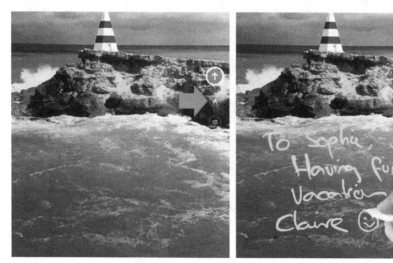

You can also add effects to a photo or video. To do this, select 'photo' from the list on the bottom right, then tap on the white/red circle to take the picture.

Once you've taken your picture, select the effects icon from the panel on the right hand side. Then select an effect from the panel that appears along the bottom.

Add some text and effects to your image. Tap and drag the effect into place.

 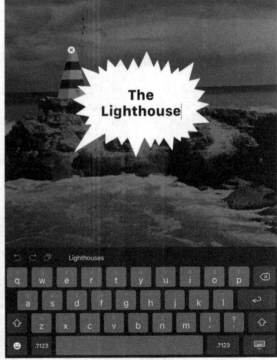

Try a few of the other effects.

Tap the blue arrow on the right hand side to send immediately, or tap 'done' on the top right of the screen to return to the message window.

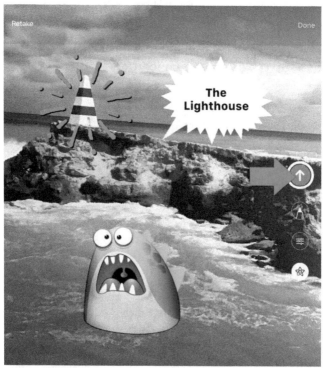

If you returned to the message window, enter a message in the text field, tap the blue arrow to the right of the text field to send.

# Digital Touch in iMessage

In digital touch mode, you can draw with your finger and send animations.

Tap the store icon to the left side of the text field to reveal additional options. Then tap the digital touch icon.

This opens up the digital touch interface. Make sure you select the digital touch icon on the bottom left. Tap the red circle on the left hand side.

This will allow you to use certain finger gestures to send different emotes. For example, you can use one finger to draw or write something, press with one finger to send a fireball effect, tap with two fingers to send a kiss and so on. Here's a list of a few of the good ones...

You can also draw using your finger, tap on a colour along the left hand side, then draw a diagram on the black screen in the centre. Press on a colour to open up the colour wheel if the colour you want isn't listed.

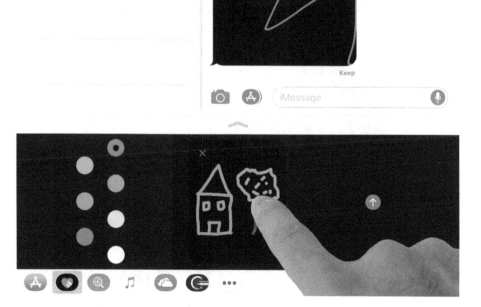

Tap on the blue arrow to the right to send.

You can also annotate a video or photograph using digital touch. To do this, from digital touch interface, tap the camera icon.

Tap the red button to start recording. While the video is recording, use the digital touch tools to draw on it. Tap a colour, then draw or write on the image with your finger.

*The white button at the bottom left takes a photo, while the red button in the centre records a video.*

Try a few 'tap and holds' with two fingers to add a few hearts. Or tap with two fingers to send a kiss.

Tap the record button again to stop recording. Tap the blue arrow at the bottom right to send your finished piece.

You can also share gifs which are short animations. Select the digital touch icon circled below. Then along the bottom of the screen, select the 'search gif' icon. Tap on a gif to add it to your message or type in to the 'find images' field to search for something specific.

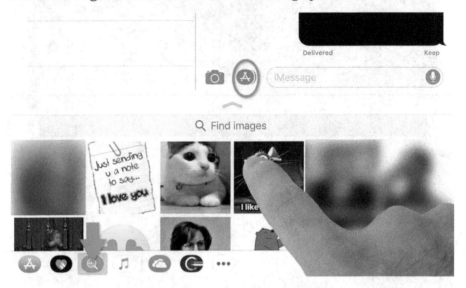

You can also share what music you are listening to on iTunes. Select the digital touch icon circled below. Then along the bottom of the screen, select the 'iTunes' icon.

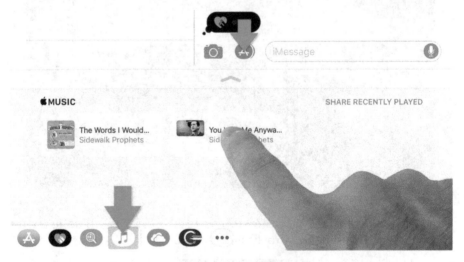

You'll see all the music you have been listening to or currently listening to on your iPad. Tap on a track to share.

# Sending Payments with iMessage

You can send payments to contacts on iMessage using Apple Pay. This only work between Apple devices at the moment, so you can't send payments to users of other phones or tablets.

Tap the store icon to the left side of the text field to reveal additional options. Then tap the Apple Pay icon.

If you have Apple Pay set up on your iPad, you'll see this icon at the bottom.

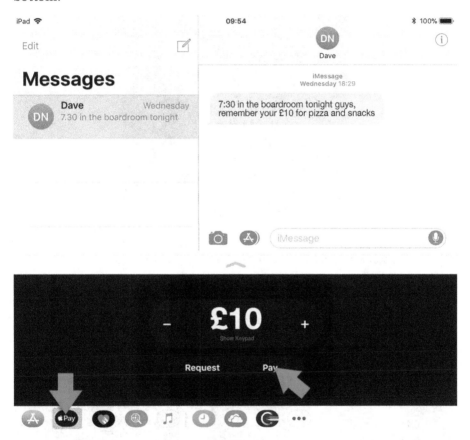

Enter the amount. Either use the + and - buttons to increase/decrease the amount, or tap 'show keypad' to tap in the amount. Once you're done hit 'pay'.

If people are owing you money, you can enter the amount as above and tap 'request' to send them an invite to pay you the amount.

# AirDrop

AirDrop allows you to transfer files from one device to another using bluetooth wireless technology.

To use AirDrop you will need a compatible device, such as the iPhone 5 or later, fourth-generation iPad, iPad mini, and fifth-generation iPod touch, and have both Bluetooth and Wi-Fi enabled.

Swipe your finger downwards from the top right edge of your screen to open control center. Tap the icons to yurn on Wi-Fi and Bluetooth.

To enable AirDrop open Control Centre and press the AirDrop icon. Make yourself discoverable to just those in your contacts.

Be careful if you select 'everyone' as this means anyone in your vicinity that has an airdrop enabled device can connect to and send files to your device, which could be a possible security risk.

## To Send a file to Someone using AirDrop

You can send a file or photo from iPhone to another iPhone or another iPad.

In this example, I am going to send a photo. So launch Photos app.

Tap the image or video you want to share from your albums, tap next.

Tap on the Share icon. AirDrop will detect other devices in the vicinity. In this example, AirDrop has detected my iPhone. This is the one I want to share with.

Tap the icon of the person/device you want to send to.

Now when you send the photo, the other person will get a prompt to download the image. Accept the confirmation and your image will download.

The image/video will be added to your photo library. The photo sent has appeared in photos app on the iPhone.

This works the same for other files too, just select the file and tap the share icon. Files will appear in the relevant apps; music will go to iTunes and files will be stored in Files app. If iOS doesn't recognise the file type, then it will ask you what app you want to open the file with.

## To Receive a File from Someone using AirDrop

Make sure your AirDrop is enabled on your device.

AirDrop will try to negotiate the connection with near by devices.

More often than not, the file will automatically download. If you get a prompt, tap on Accept when the photo comes through

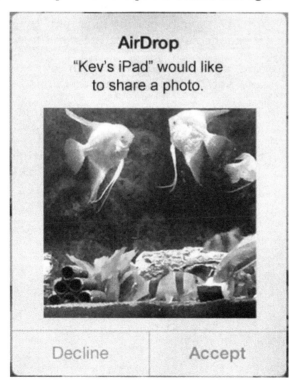

Go into your photos app and the photo will be stored in there.

**149**

# Using Multimedia

Your iPad is a multimedia rich device, meaning you can take photos and record videos. You can even edit and enhance your photos, correct colour and brightness.

You can post your photographs to your favourite social media account for the world to see.

You can create slide shows, edit your videos, download and watch TV programmes and films.

You can download and play any kind of music you can think of, all from your iPad.

So lets begin by taking a look at the Photos App.

# Photos

Using the photos app, you can import photos from a memory card or digital camera, edit and share photos taken with the on board cameras on your iPad.

## Import Photos

There are two adapters available to accomplish this: the Lightning to SD Card Reader, or the Lightning to USB Adapter.

The card reader enables you to insert the SD card from your camera and copy images from it.

The card reader plugs into the docking port on the bottom of the iPad. Launch the iPhoto app. Tap on camera or card.

You can also connect your camera directly using a lightning to USB connector. Plug the connector into the bottom of your iPad, then plug the USB cable that came with your camera into the other end of the lightning to USB adapter.

When iPad detects your media, it will prompt you with an import screen. Tap the photographs you want to import and then tap import to copy the photos across.

Once the photos have been imported, you will see a prompt asking you whether to keep the images or delete them.

If you select keep, this leaves all the photos intact on the memory card. If you select delete, this deletes the photos you just imported off the memory card.

Once all the photos have been imported it is safe to delete the photos off the card.

# Editing Photos

You can do some basic editing on your iPad. You can lighten up dark images, crop and rotate your photos.

To do this tap on the photograph in the photos app.

The image will open up full screen. Tap on the edit icon on the top right of the screen.

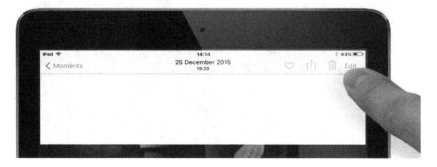

Along the bottom of the screen you'll see your editing icons.

Reading the icons in the centre from left to right we have:

**Image enhance**, this automatically selects the brightness, colour and contrast settings for your photograph. Most of the time it is a guess based on optimal settings but doesn't always get it right.

**Image crop and rotate,** this allows you to rotate images that may have been taken at an angle or crop parts of the photo you don't want.

**Effects,** allows you to add black and white, fade, sepia effects to a photo.

**Adjustments,** allows you to adjust colour, brightness, contrast, bring up shadows, reduce highlights in bright areas of a photo

# Crop and Rotate an Image

You can crop an image by tapping on the crop image icon, circled below, and dragging the crop box around the bit of the photo you want.

If you want to rotate the image, tap and drag the rotation protractor underneath the image to the left or right.

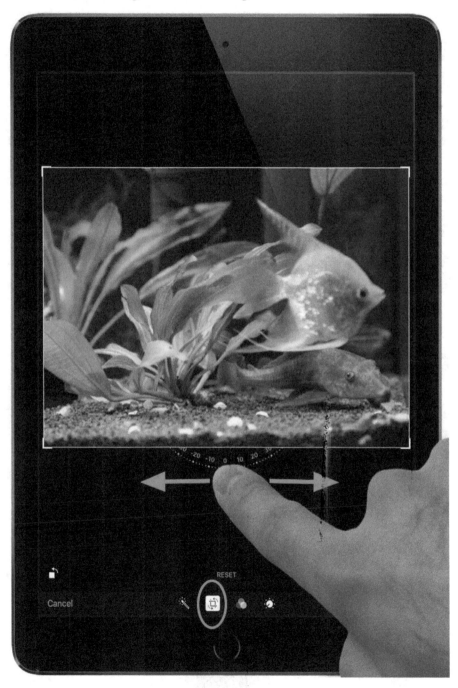

If you want to correct colour, contrast or brightness, tap the adjustments icon, circled below.

In this example I am going to adjust the brightness of the photo. So tap on 'light'.

The 'light' group contains everything to do with exposure: brightness, contrast, highlights, shadows etc.

Drag the slider with your finger, left and right, to adjust the brightness. To change contrast or highlights, tap the hamburger icon to the right.

From the menu, select the one you want to change - try adjusting highlights - this is the bright parts of the image. Also try adjust the contrast.

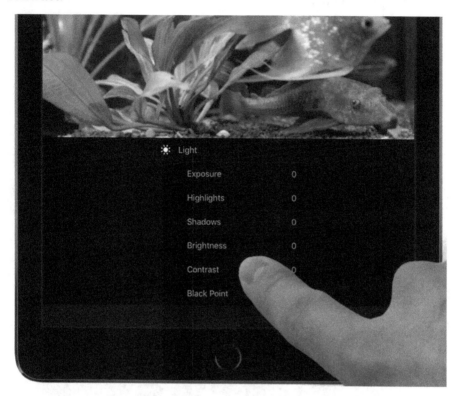

Use the slider to change the setting.

Take a look at the 'adjusting photos' video demo in the 'multimedia' section of the accompanying resources. Scan code or go to following website.

www.elluminetpress.com/ipad-mm

# Taking Pictures with Camera App

Tap the camera icon on the home screen.

You can use your iPad as a camera to take photos and record video.

Along the right side of your screen you have some icons. With the top icon, you can enable HDR (this is good for scenes where you have dark shadows and bright areas such as sky). Next down is a timer delay (can set to off, 3 or 10 seconds). Third icon down swaps between front and rear camera. The white circle takes the photo, the thumbnail icon underneath shows you the last photo taken. Underneath this you can select the type of video or photo you want to take: time lapse, slomo, video, photo, square photo and panoramic photo. You can select them by swiping your finger over them.

**158**

You can adjust the zoom using the slider on the left hand side of the image. Drag the circle on the bar upwards to zoom in, and downwards to zoom out.

If you're having trouble focusing, tap and hold your finger on the object you want to focus on. This will lock the exposure and focus on that object, so it doesn't change, making it easier to take the photo.

Tap the white circle on the right hand side as normal to take the photo

You can also adjust the brightness before you take a photo. To do this tap on the screen and you'll see a yellow square show up with a vertical line with a slider on it.

Drag the slider upward to brighten up the image, slide it downward to darken the image.

Tap the white circle to take the photo as normal.

Take a look at the 'taking photos' video demo in the 'multimedia' section of the accompanying resources. Scan code or go to following website.

www.elluminetpress.com/ipad-mm

# Adjusting Photos

Once you have taken your photo you can you can crop or rotate the image. Rotating an image is good for straightening up photos.

To crop the image, tap the photo icon on the right hand side of the screen, to open the photo you just took.

Use the grid shown below to highlight the section of the photograph you want to keep. Drag the edges of the box inwards to the point you want to crop

You can straighten a photograph by rotating it a number of degrees. To do this drag the dials up and down on the left hand side of the screen.

You can also change the shading and tonal effects of the image, making your image black and white, a sepia effect or boost the colours.

Tap the photo icon on the right hand side of the screen, to open the photo you just took.

Now tap edit on the top right of your screen. To add tonal effects, tap the colour icon at the bottom of your screen.

You can adjust the brightness and contrast or highlight shadows where photographs have come out dark in places.

You can do this by tapping on the light adjust icon. This is the same as adjusting your photos in the photos app.

From the options, select the attributes of the photo you want to adjust, this is the exposure, highlights, shadows, brightness, contrast, or black point.

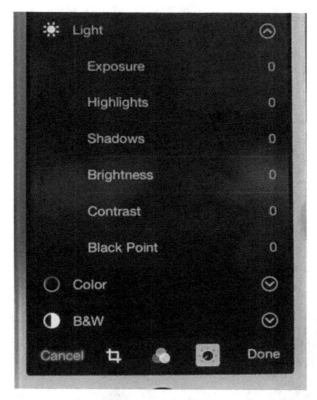

For example, tap on highlights to darken some of the bright parts in your image.

Drag the bar left and right to change the highlight.

Also try exposure or brightness to lighten a dark image or shadows to lighten up dark parts of an image.

## Panoramic Photos

Panoramic shots are great for scenery and landscapes. Photos app allows you to automatically take a series of photos and it stitches them together into a long panoramic image.

To take panoramic photos, open your camera app, select pano from the right hand side of the screen. You might need to scroll down the selections if it isn't visible.

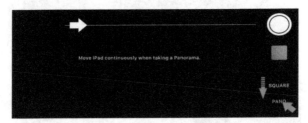

Now, move your iPad to the start of the scene and tap the white circle. You'll notice in the centre of the screen a rectangular box, this will start to fill as you move your iPad across the scene. In this demonstration, I'm taking a panoramic photo of a mountain range.

Position your iPad camera at the beginning of the mountain range on the left, tap the white 'take photo' icon on the right of your screen. Now move your camera along the mountain range until you get to the end. You'll see the rectangular box in the centre of the screen fill up as you do so. Tap the white circle again to finish. Make sure you stand in one spot, the panoramic photos don't work if you walk along with it.

# Recording Video

You can record video using the camera app. Select 'video' from the list on the bottom right of your screen.

To take the best looking video, use your iPad in a horizontal orientation as shown below.

Tap the red circle icon on the right hand side of the screen to start recording. Tap on any part of the screen to focus on that point during the video. Use the slider on the left hand side to zoom in and out. Tap the red circle icon on the right hand side to stop recording.

Take a look at the 'recording video' demo in the 'multimedia' section of the accompanying resources.

www.elluminetpress.com/ipad-mm

## Live Photos

Live Photos capture 1.5 seconds of motion before and after the photo.

To take a live photo, from the Camera app, tap the Live Photo button, right at the top of the screen to turn it on, indicated with the red arrow below.

Tap the Shutter button to take your Live Photo.

They animate when you press firmly and hold your finger on the photo. To see your live photos in the photos app, tap on the photo thumbnail in the main screen.

Then when the photo opens up, press your finger firmly on the photo to see the animation.

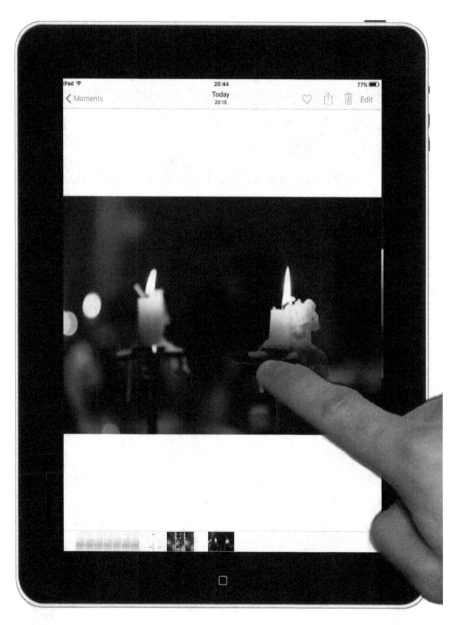

## Share Pics on Social Media

You will need to be logged into, and downloaded the appropriate app from the app store; facebook or twitter etc.

In this example I'm going to share a photograph on Facebook of the twins.

If you have taken the photo using your camera, tap the small thumbnail in the bottom right hand corner. *If you're in the photos app, tap on your photograph thumbnail to open it in edit mode.*

Once the photo opens up, tap the share icon in the top right corner.

Select 'Facebook' from the list of social media icons.

## Chapter 5: Using Multimedia

Type a message in your post, then hit 'post'.

You can use the same procedure for Twitter, email iMessage and any other social media you use. Just select the icon from the social media icons list

# Music with iTunes

You can start the music app by tapping on music icon on the main screen.

Once music app has loaded you can see all the albums that are currently on your iPad

Tapping on the album cover brings up the song list. Just tap the song on the song list and it will start playing. Time to put on your headphones.

# Connecting to your Computer

To get music onto iPad you can purchase and download from the iTunes Store or sync with iTunes on your computer, by connecting your iPad using the iPad USB cable.

Open iTunes on your computer and click the iPad/iPhone icon on the top right of the tool bar.

Here you can update your iPad's iOS software, just click 'check for update'. Press the option key and click 'check for updates' if you have downloaded a restore image (IPSW).

You can restore your device to its factory settings if you have problems with it. To do this click 'restore iPhone/iPad'. This will wipe your data, apps, music and settings, so you'll need to restore from a backup if you do this.

Further down the options, you can set backups. By default, your data is automatically backed up to your iCloud account, but you can also set it to backup to your computer - this means you'd have to plug your device into your computer to allow this. Most of the time leaving this backing up to iCloud is sufficient.

Scroll down to the bottom of this page and select **'manually manage music and videos'**. This allows you to select the songs or albums you want to transfer instead of syncing your whole library.

Options

☑ Open iTunes when this iPad is connected

☐ Sync with this iPad over Wi-Fi

☐ Sync only checked songs and videos

☐ Prefer standard definition videos

☐ Convert higher bit rate songs to   128 kbps ⬍   AAC

☑ Manually manage music and videos

Reset Warnings

Configure Accessibility...

26.29 GB Free

## Transferring Music

Enable your sidebar in iTunes, if it isn't already open. I find this helps when transferring songs or albums to an iPad. To do this, open the view menu and select 'show sidebar'.

Also your iPad will need to be set to 'manually manage music and videos' - see previous section on how to do this.

Now select 'music' from the 'library' on the top left.

To add any music to your iPad, just drag and drop the track or album onto the iPad device shown in the left hand sidebar.

Take a look at the 'adding music to iPad' demos in the multimedia section of the accompanying video resources. Scan code or go to following website.

www.elluminetpress.com/ipad-mm

# iTunes Store

You can start the iTunes store by tapping on the icon on your home screen

Once the app has loaded you can browse through music, movies and tv shows by tapping on the icons. You can also type what you are looking for in the search field on the top right of the screen.

To buy any of the tracks or albums, tap your finger on the price tag.

You will need your Apple ID to buy any of the media.

# Apple Music

Apple Music is a music streaming service that allows you to stream music from the iTunes music library for a monthly subscription fee.

- £4.99 a month gives you full access to the iTunes music library and is only available for University/College students.

- £9.99 a month gets you full access to the iTunes music library and many radio stations available. This is an individual account and allows only one account access to the iTunes Store.

- £14.99 a month gets you full access to the iTunes music library and radio stations and allows up to 6 people to sign in and listen to their music. This is ideal for families.

## Setting Up

Open iTunes Music App and from the list of icons along the bottom of the screen, select 'for you'.

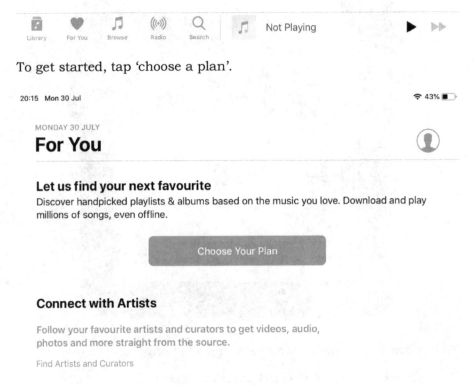

To get started, tap 'choose a plan'.

Choose a membership programme, then tap 'join apple music'.

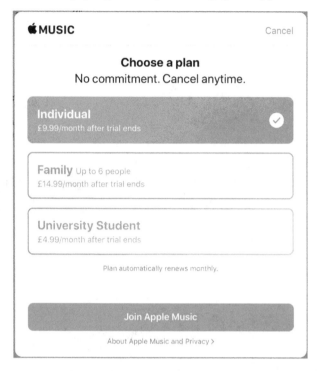

Enter your Apple ID username and password, or confirm with touch ID, if you have this enabled, by placing your finger on the home button.

Tap the genres you like. Tap 'next' when you're done.

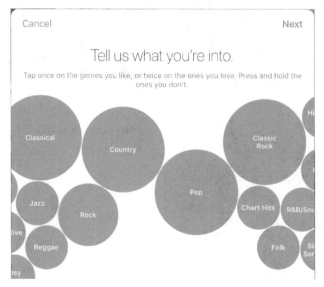

## The Main Screen

You can use the icons along the bottom of Apple Music to navigate around.

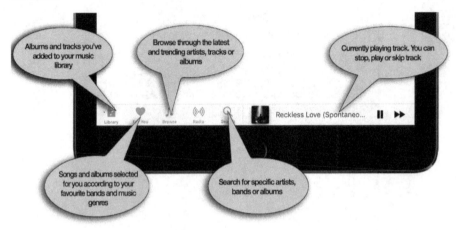

Tap the currently playing track to reveal the album or track details

# Searching for Music

Select the artists you like. If you don't see all the ones you like, tap 'more artists' on the bottom left. If the artist you're looking for isn't there, you can add them. To do this tap 'add an artist' and enter their name.

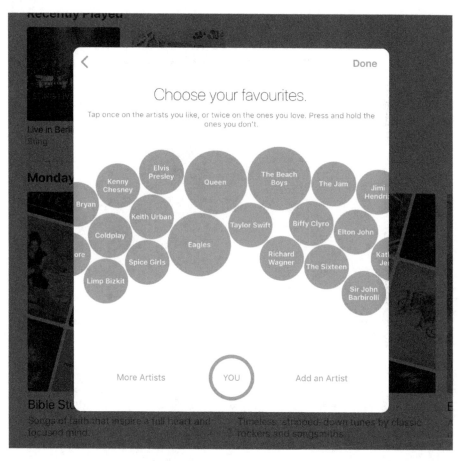

Now, you can search for any artist, band or song you can think of. To do this, on Apple iTunes Music's home screen, select 'search' from the icons along the bottom of the screen.

Type an artist's/album name into the search field at the top.

Select the closest match from the list of suggestions.

From here you can tap on a song to listen to it, open an album, add to your music library, or you can build your own playlists.

Tap on an album to open it.

## Add to Library

You can start to create a library of your favourite music, so it's easy to find. To do this, tap the + sign next to the song you want to add to your library. If you want to add the whole album tap '+add'.

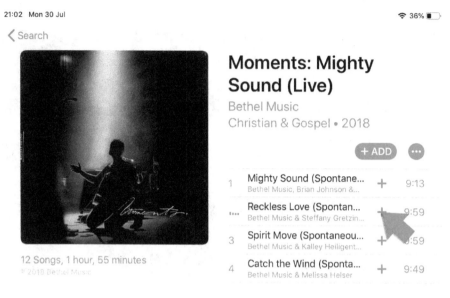

You can access your music library using the 'library' icon on the bar along the bottom of the screen.

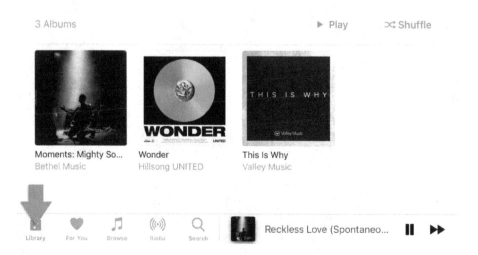

Tap an album to open it, tap on a track to play it

# Films & TV

You can stream films and TV programmes directly to your iPad from the iTunes Store. You can buy or rent what you want to watch. To to this, select 'films' or 'tv programmes' from the panel along the bottom of the screen.

You can also search for a specific title using the search field at the top right of the screen, or to browse your favourite genre, tap 'genres' on the top left.

Search for a film or TV programme you want to watch either by typing the title into the search or browse through the genres. Tap on the thumbnail cover to view the details.

On the film details screen you'll be able to read details about the film, reviews and ratings. Tap 'rent' or 'buy'. Verify your purchase using the Touch ID, or your Apple ID username and password.

You'll find your downloaded films and TV programmes in the library section of the TV App.

# TV App

The TV App is where you'll find all your purchased or rented films and TV programmes. You'll find the app on your home screen.

Select 'library' from the panel along the bottom of the screen.

Tap on the film or tv programme to begin playback.

**183**

# Airplay

Airplay allows wireless streaming of audio and video data to an Apple TV or compatible receiver on your TV.

For this to work, both your iPad and Apple TV will need to be on the same WiFi network. This is usually the case in most homes.

To mirror your iPad, open your control centre - swipe downwards from the top right edge of your screen.

Tap on 'screen mirroring' or 'airplay mirroring' and select your Apple TV from the list. Enter your passcode if prompted.

If you don't know the Apple TV passcode, go on your Apple TV, then go to settings > Airplay, select 'Onscreen code'.

You can turn off the code or set a new one.

# Apple Pencil

If you have an iPad pro or the iPad 9.7" model, then you can use the Apple Pencil.

You'll need to purchase an Apple Pencil to use this feature. You can order it directly from Apple's website.

Use your pencil on Pages, Keynote, Microsoft Word, Excel and PowerPoint to add annotations and handwritten notes.

There are also some artistic apps where you can apply pressure to create darker lines or tilt your pencil to shade in areas.

Just type 'apple pencil' into the search field in the app store and you'll find plenty of apps.

Take a look at the apple pencil video demos in the multimedia section of the resources. Scan code or go to following website.

www.elluminetpress.com/ipad-mm

# Charge your Pencil

First you should charge up your pencil. To do this, pull the small white cap off the back of your pencil.

You can charge your pencil using the iPad charger. First plug the lightning adapter onto the end of the pencil making sure the small circle on the adapter is facing the pencil. Then plug the cable from your iPad charger into the other end of the lightning adapter.

You can also plug the pencil into the lightning port on the bottom on your iPad. Leave it plugged in for a short while to give it some charge.

# Pairing your Pencil with your iPad

Make sure your pencil is charged up and your iPad is powered on. Plug your pencil into the lightning port on the bottom of your iPad.

On your iPad, you'll see a prompt. Tap 'turn on' if your bluetooth is off.

On the next prompt tap 'pair'.

This will connect your pencil to your iPad. Once this is done, you can use your pencil on your iPad

# Using Apple Pencil

You can use apple pencil to take hand written notes. Open up the notes app.

Along the bottom right of the screen you'll see three icons. Tap the markup icon on the far right.

You can write directly onto the surface of your iPad.

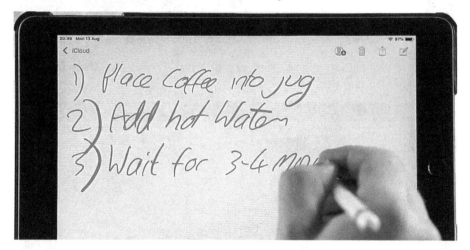

Use the icons on the markup toolbar to select a pen type: marker, highlighter, pencil, eraser and lasso tool, as well as a colour and thickness and opacity (how dark or light the pen is).

# Chapter 5: Using Multimedia

You can also highlight and annotate using your favourite productivity apps. In Microsoft Word, select the 'draw' ribbon, select a pen and draw directly onto the document. In Pages, you can draw directly onto the iPad screen on an open document with your pencil - the markup toolbar will appear along the bottom of the screen.

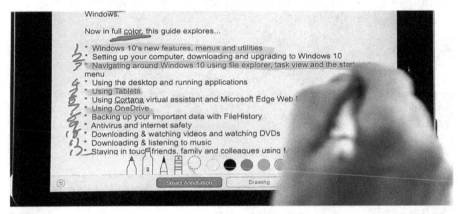

If you are an artist or designer, try out the **Concepts Drawing App** available from the app store.

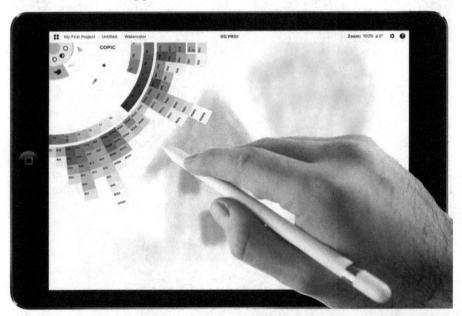

Have a look at the pencil demos in the multimedia section of the video resources. Scan code or go to following website.

www.elluminetpress.com/ipad-mm

# Document Scanner

Within the Notes App, you can scan documents and convert them. From the Notes App, tap the + sign on the bottom right of your screen.

Tap 'manual' on the right hand side, this is so you can take a photo of each of your pages and gives you more control than auto mode.

Line up the document in the window as shown below, make sure the yellow box covers the whole document.

Tap the white button on the right hand side to 'scan the document'. If you have more pages, repeat the process and 'scan' them as well using the white button on the right hand side. Once you have 'scanned' all your pages, tap 'save' on the bottom right corner.

The pages will be added to your note. Tap on the thumbnail to open it up full screen.

Now you can send the document via email, safe it as a PDF, print it and write directly onto the scan with markup.

Tap the 'share' icon on the top right of your screen.

In this demonstration, I'm going to add some annotations with the markup tool. So tap 'markup'.

Select a pen or highlighter from the selection at the bottom left, and select a colour from the bottom right.

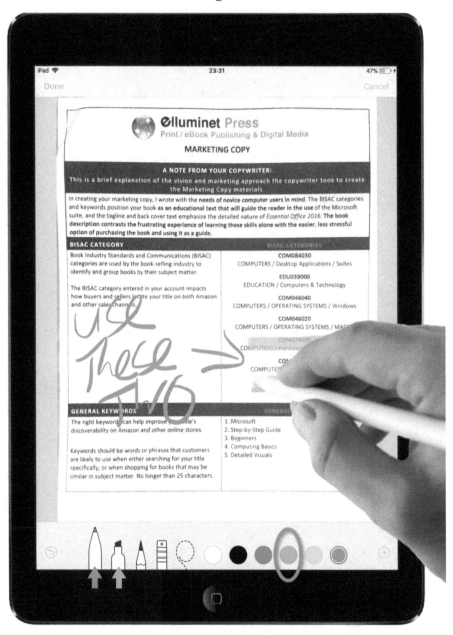

Use your finger or pen to draw directly onto the scanned document.

When you're done, tap 'done' on the top left.

# Chapter 5: Using Multimedia

Now to send it or save it, tap the 'share' icon on the top right of the screen.

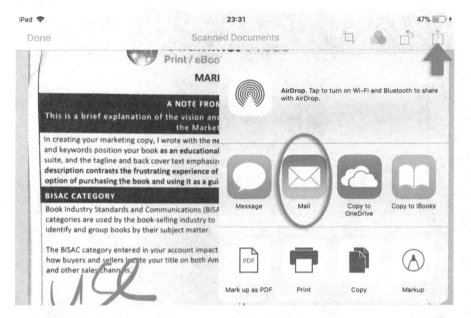

From the drop down, tap 'mail' to email it to someone or 'message' to send via iMessage. From here you can also save it to a PDF or print it if you have air print installed. In this example I'm emailing it.

# QR Code Scanner

Open your camera app, point it at a QR code, tap the code on the screen to focus.

When the camera reads the code, you'll see a prompt at the top of the screen telling you what the code is and where it links to. Tap and drag the small handle, circled above, down to expand the window to see a preview of the website. Tap on the site to open it up in full screen.

# Common Apps

You can pretty much get an app for virtually anything, and these are all available from the app store. Some are free and others you have to buy.

There are games, productivity apps and apps just for fun.

Your iPad comes with some apps build in but you can download millions more from the App Store.

Lets start by taking a look at the App Store in more detail.

The App Store has had a make over in this version of iOS and has a much easier to use interface

# App Store

The app store has over 1 million apps available for download direct to your iPad without even going on a computer. To start app store, click App Store app on your main screen.

Once on the app store's main screen, tap the icon on the top right to sign in with your Apple ID if you haven't already done so. If you are already signed in, your Apple ID will be displayed here, you won't need to sign in again.

# Apps

TRY SOMETHING NEW                    TRY SOMETHING NEW
Bloom - Colouring Book               Farfetch – Shop & Discover Desig...   B
Your real world colour palette       Shop the latest trends               W

In the box that appears, enter your Apple ID details.

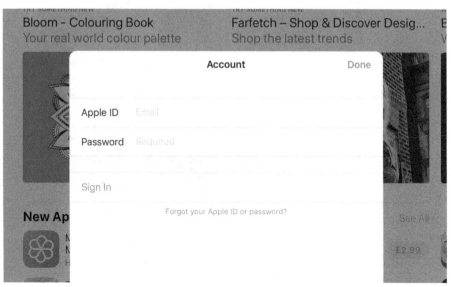

## Chapter 6: Common Apps

On the app store, you will find everything from games and entertainment to productivity tools such as word processing, drawing and photo apps.

These are split into games and app sections and you'll find these on the bar along the bottom of the screen.

Also along the bottom you'll find updates to your installed apps, it's worth checking this from time to time, as apps are updated all the time.

The last icon on the bar along the bottom allows you to search the app store for a specific app name or type/genre of app.

You can even find apps for recipes, travel details, maps. There is an app for almost anything you can think of.

# Search for Apps

To find an app, tap on 'search' on the bar at the bottom of your screen. Type into the search field on the main screen, as shown below. In this example, I'm going to search for one of my favourite games called 'worms'.

From the suggestions, tap on the closest match. Tap on the image to view more details about the app; here you'll see reviews, price, screen shots and other info.

To download the app, tap 'get' next to the app if it's free, or tap the price tag if it's paid.

If it's a paid app, tap 'purchase' to confirm.

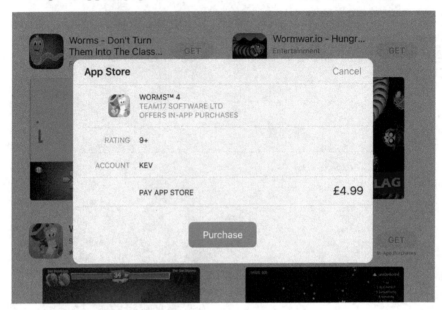

Authorise the purchase with your Apple ID password or if you have touch ID setup, with your thumb print.

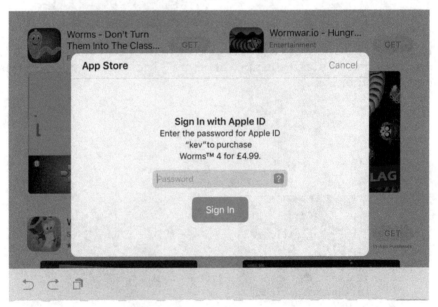

The app will appear on your home screen once it has downloaded and installed itself.

## Browsing the Store

If you are more the browsing type, app store has grouped all the apps into categories according to their use. Select 'apps' from the bar on the bottom of the screen. Here you'll see some of the most popular apps, new apps and top selling apps. You can tap on any of these apps to view or download.

Tap on the app's image to view more details, Tap 'see all' at the top of each section to see all the apps in that section. Tap on 'get' or the price to download the app. Scroll down the page to see all the apps in the sections.

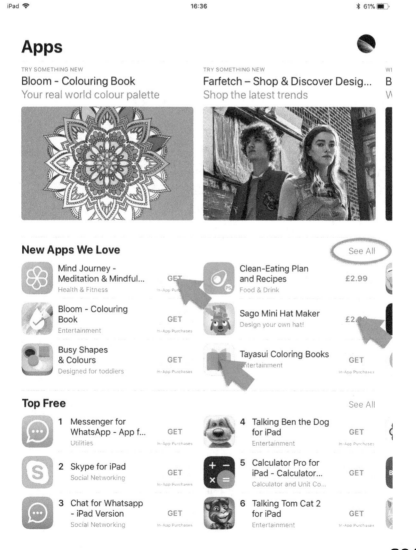

# Chapter 6: Common Apps

If you scroll down a bit, you'll see a section called 'top categories'.

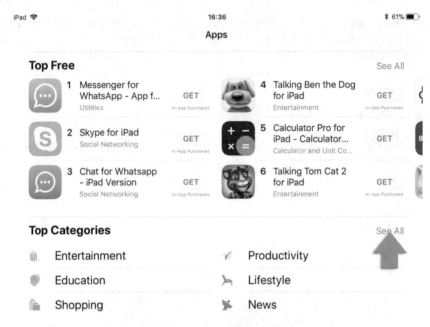

Tap on a category to browse the available apps. In this example, I'm going to explore the 'reference' category.

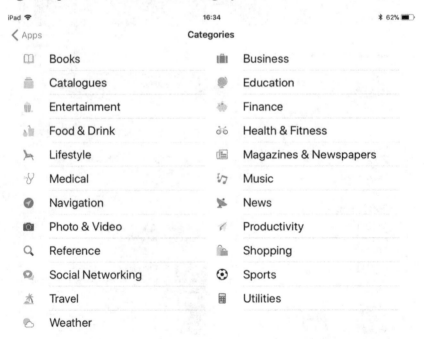

Here, you'll see a list of all the apps available for that category. Again, tap 'see all' on the top right to see the full lists in the different sections.

Claire is 18 and learning to drive, so two apps might be of use to her: Theory Test and Hazard Perception. Tap on the apps icon to view more details about the app

Tap the price to download the and install the app on your iPad

This gives you information about what the app does, what it costs, some screen shots of the app in action and the device requirements in order to run the app.

To purchase an app, just tap on the price tag.

# Taking Notes

To start notes app, tap on the icon on the home screen.

When notes has loaded, you can view your saved notes along the left hand side. You can add a new note by tapping the pen and pad icon on the top right.

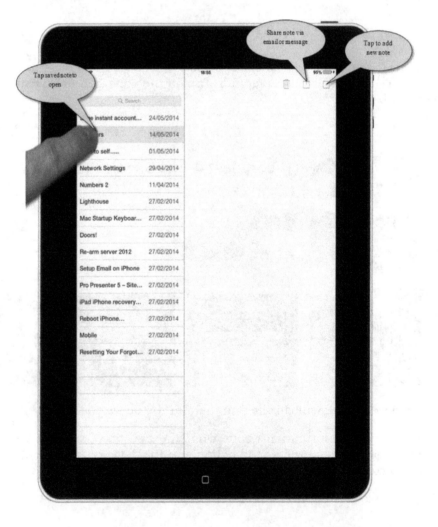

## Typing Notes & Inserting Photos

You can type your notes in as if it were a notepad, using the on screen keyboard.

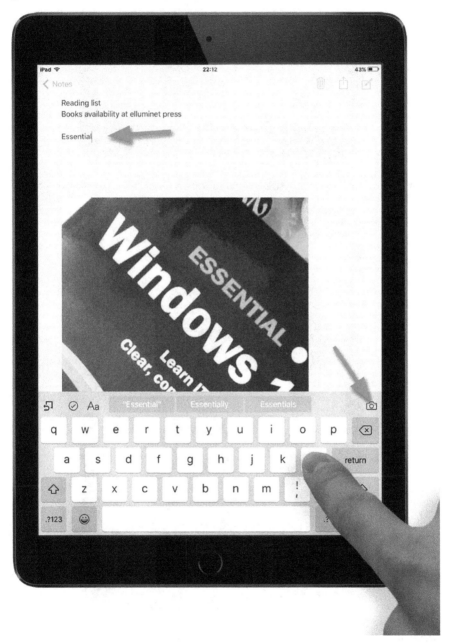

You can also insert a photograph by tapping on the small camera icon.

## Dictating Notes

Instead of typing, you can dictate notes using the voice dictation feature. To do this, tap the mic icon on the keyboard.

Record your notes using the voice recognition.

Tap done at the bottom, when you are finished.

# Reminders

To start reminders app, tap on the icon on the home screen

## Add a Reminder

To add one, tap reminders (on the left hand side), tap on a blank line on the paper then type your reminder.

Tap return on the keyboard to add another reminder. These are reminders of things to do today.

## Schedule a Reminder

To schedule reminders, tap scheduled on the left hand side of the screen

Add a reminder by tapping on a blank line and entering a description of the task.

Then tap the 'i' icon on the right hand side of the reminder

This will allow you to enter the date and time. Tap 'alarm' then swipe up and down the days and times that appear, shown below.

# Maps

Maps is an extremely useful app if you are trying to find out where a particular place is and need to find driving directions. It works like a SatNav/GPS giving you precise directions straight from door to door.

You can view the map in three different types - tap the 'i' icon on the top right of the screen to change this.

**Street maps** are great if you are using the maps app as a GPS/Satnav while driving, **transit maps** give you public transport routes in a particular location, and **satellite maps** are great if you are exploring a city or area of interest.

# Driving Directions

To find driving directions, type in your destination into the search field on the top left of the screen and select the destination from the list of suggestions.

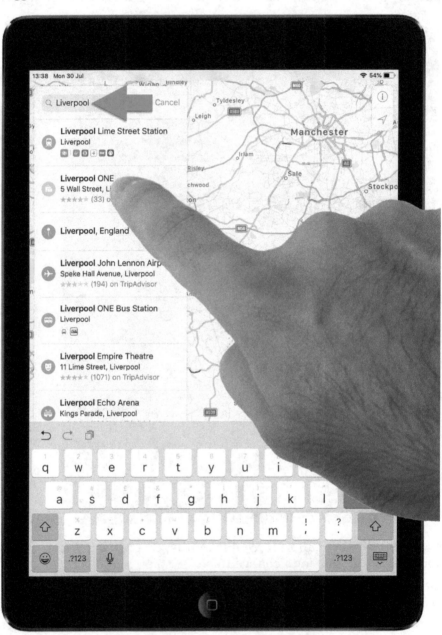

Select 'directions' from the destination sidebar.

By default, the maps app will start the route from your current location - you can change this, just type in another location.

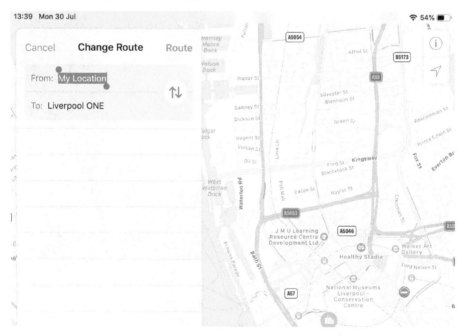

Tap on 'route' to calculate a route between your location and the destination you entered earlier.

# Chapter 6: Common Apps

Along the bottom of the screen, you'll see 'drive', 'walk', and 'transport'. This allows you to get directions for driving, if you're walking, or if you're taking public transport. For this demo, we're looking for driving directions, so we'll keep the option set to 'drive'.

On the screen you'll see an overview of your route. You can zoom in and out or move around the map using your finger to see details or roads.

From options on the left hand side of the screen, select the best route if there is more than one route.

Here you'll see the start of your route, with turn by turn directions that will automatically change as you drive along the route.

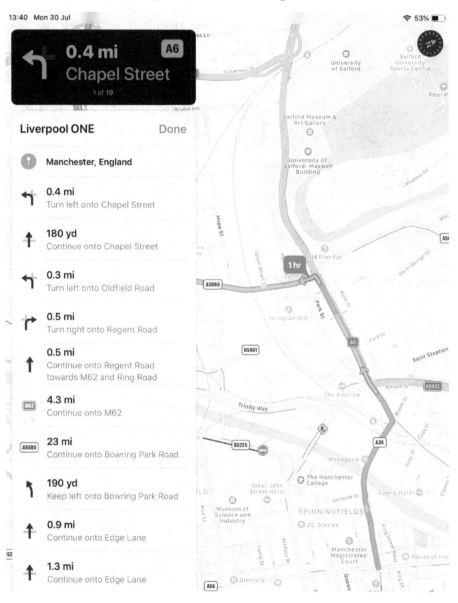

Take a look at the 'Exploring Maps' demo in the 'using iPad' section of the accompanying video resources. Scan the code or go to the following website

www.elluminetpress.com/using-ipad

# 3D Maps

3D maps are a great way to explore landmarks, major cities and areas of interest. You can flyover a city and explore what it has to offer.

To do this, first change your map to a satellite map if you haven't already done so. Then tap the 3D icon on the right hand side to switch to 3D mode.

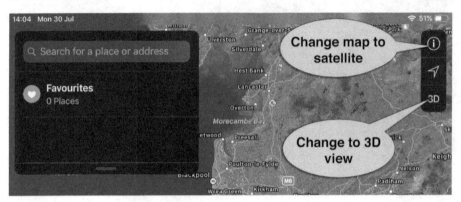

Type in a city name, place name or address into the search field on the top left of the screen.

You can zoom in and out of the 3D map and move around using your finger

To take a flyover tour, tap 'flyover' in the info side panel.

Now move your iPad around, as you do this you'll notice the view move on your iPad. Use your finger to zoom in and out or move up and down the view.

Tap once anywhere on the screen to reveal the popup menu on the bottom left.

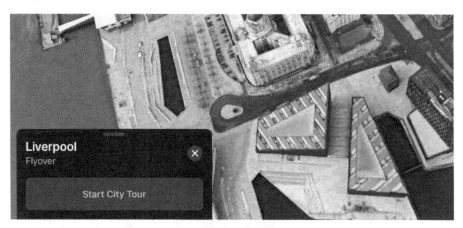

Tap 'start city tour' if available for that city to watch an animated 3D tour of the city.

Tap the x to close the flyover view.

# News App

The news app collects breaking stories from around the world and locally into one app, based on the topics you are interested in.

When you first start the app, you'll see a list of top stories, trending stories, and stories recommended for you. Scroll down the page, tap on a story to read the details.

To open the side panel, tap the icon on the top left of the screen

From here you can select different news sources, magazines, newspapers and websites.

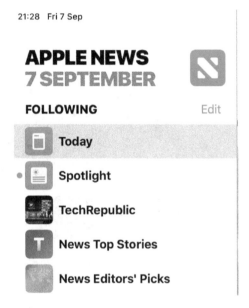

You can also search for specific channels. To reveal the search field if it isn't already visible, swipe downwards on the side panel, the search field will appear at the top. Type in your search.

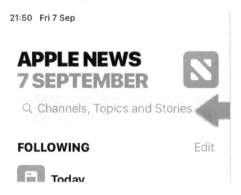

# Apple Books App

Formerly known as iBooks, Apple Books is your electronic bookshelf and allows you to read ebooks. Tap the icon on your home screen.

You can download hundreds of different e-books that are available in the bookstore; from the latest novels, food, kids books or manuals.

Along the bottom of the screen you'll see some icons. Here you can see the books you are 'reading now', browse your library of books you've downloaded, browse the book store, look at audio books and search for a specific book title or author.

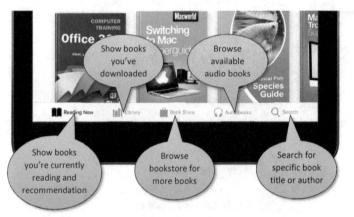

Just tap on the book cover to open the book.

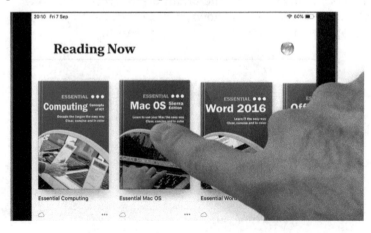

You can also browse through the book store. To do this, tap 'bookstore' icon on the panel along the bottom of the screen.

Click 'browse sections' to reveal the categories in the bookstore. Now select a category. Perhaps you're into 'crime thrillers', 'fiction', or 'education'. Just tap on a category to view the available books.

You can also search for specific authors or titles. To do this tap on the 'search' icon on the panel along the bottom of the screen.

Then type what you're looking for in the search field at the top of the screen.

Tap on a book cover to see more details.

From this page you'll be able to read a sample, the book's description, read any reviews, and buy/download the book.

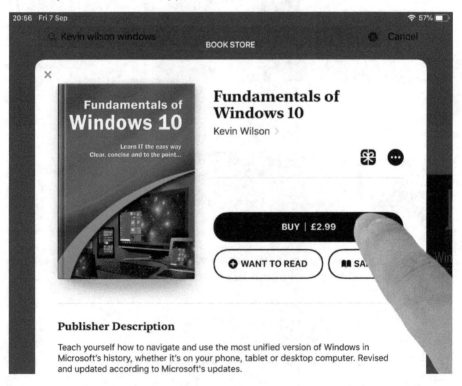

Tap 'get' if the book is free, or tap the price tag to download the book to your library.

Once you've downloaded the book, you'll find it in your library. Tap the library icon on the panel along the bottom of the screen.

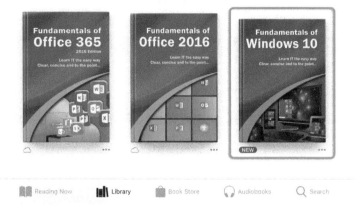

Tap on the book cover to begin reading.

# Files App

The iCloud Drive App has been dropped and replaced with the Files App. You'll find the icon on your dock, as shown below.

In the Files App, you'll find all your files that are stored on your iPad and iCloud Drive. Here is the Files App opened in horizontal mode.

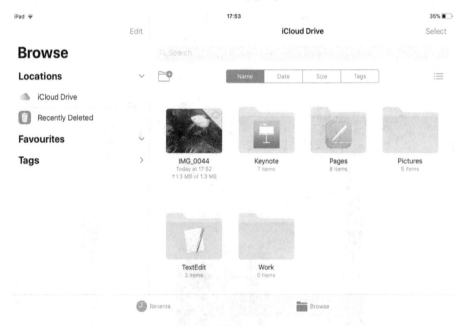

When working with any of Apple's productivity apps such as Keynote, Pages or Numbers, the files you create will be saved into the appropriate folders in the Files App.

You can also create your own folders. To do this tap the 'new folder' icon on the top left.

You can drag and drop files into these folders. Tap and hold your finger on the icon, then drag your finger across the glass to the folder you want to put the file into.

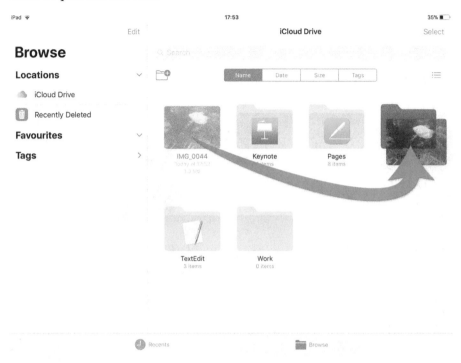

Tap on the folders to open them, tap on the file thumbnails to open the files.

You can also delete files. Tap and hold your finger on the file thumbnail and from the pop up menu tap 'delete'.

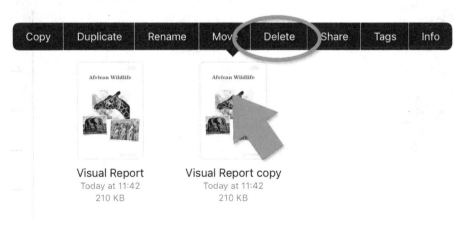

As an example, I am going to save a document from the Pages App. To make sure you're saving into iCloud Drive, from the start screen, tap 'location' on the top left. From the drop down select 'browse'.

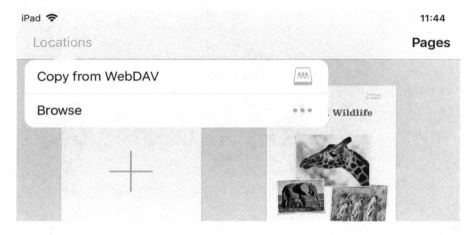

Tap 'locations', then tap 'iCloud Drive. Tap 'browse'.

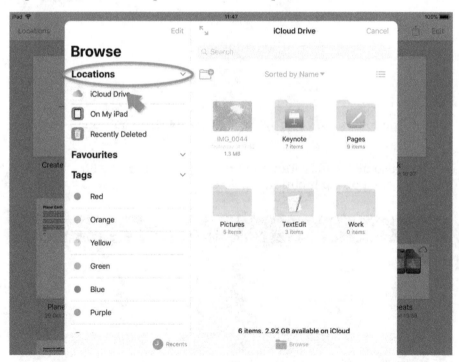

Tap the 'Pages' folder. Now you'll see all the files that have been saved in this folder.

'Pages' files are automatically saved here.

# Apple Pay

Apple Pay allows you to keep digital copies of your bank cards, and lets you pay for things using your iPhone or iPad. You can use this feature on an iPad but it is more convenient with an iPhone.

*Apple Pay will run on iPhone SE, iPhone 6, iPhone 6 Plus, and later as well as, iPad Pro, iPad Air 2, iPad mini 3, and later.*

## Setup

Make sure your bank supports Apple Pay. If so, go to your settings app then scroll down the left hand side and tap 'wallet & apple pay'. Then tap 'add credit or debit card' link. Tap 'continue' on the apple pay popup.

Now, in the 'add card' window, if you already have a credit/debit card registered with your Apple ID, then apple pay will ask you to add this one.

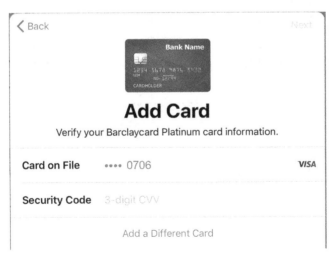

If this is the card you want to use, then enter the 3 digit security code and tap 'next' on the top right. Hit 'agree' on the terms and conditions; your card will be added.

If you want to add a different card, tap 'add a different card', at the bottom of the 'add card' window. You can scan your card with the iPad's camera.

Position the card so it fills the white rectangle on your screen. Apple Pay will scan your card and automatically enter your details

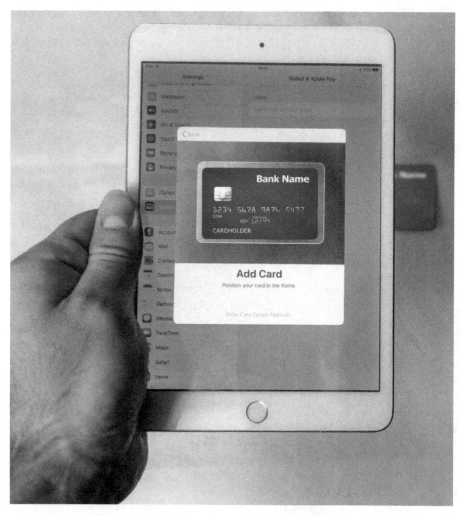

If you can't get the camera to scan the card, tap 'enter card details manually' then key in your card number, exp dates and so on.

Enter the security code from the back of your card. The bank will authorise your card. Accept the terms and conditions.

If you also have an iPhone, these cards will be synced with your iPhone so you can use Apple Pay on there too.

# Using Apple Pay

You can use Apple Pay at any store that supports this feature. You will usually see the logo displayed in store. You can also use Apple Pay on some online stores.

To pay with Apple Pay, place your iPhone/iPad above the reader with your thumb on the home button without pressing it. You'll see a prompt on your iPhone for the amount - you authorise the payment using the finger print scanner on the home button.

If you want to pay with a card other than the default, hold the top of your iPhone near the contactless reader without touching the home button.

Tap the card you want to use.

Present your iPhone to the contactless reader with your thumb on the home button to complete payment.

Holding your thumb on the home button uses the finger print reader to verify your identity and is sometimes called 'touch id'.

# Voice Memos

You can record audio using your iPad's built in mic or a bluetooth external mic. You can record voice memos, meetings and lectures.

You'll find the voice memo app on your home screen.

Lets take a look at the main screen. Here you can see your previous recordings listed down the left hand side. Any recording you select here will appear in the white panel on the right hand side of the screen.

Tap the play button in the grey panel on the right to playback the recording.

## Recording Memos

To record a memo, simply tap the red record button on the bottom left of the screen.

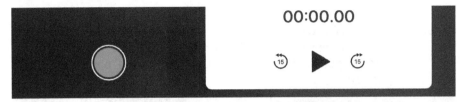

The memo app will start recording. You'll see a wave form appear in the middle of the screen to indicate the app is picking up audio.

To pause a recording temporarily, tap the pause icon on the left. To stop the recording, tap 'done'.

Your memo will appear in the list on the left hand side of the main screen.

## Renaming Memos

The first thing you should do with a new voice memo recording is give it a meaningful name. The last thing you want is every memo called 'new recording.

To demonstrate this, we'll rename the voice memo we just recorded. Select the voice memo from the list on the left hand side. Then tap and hold your finger on the name in the right hand panel, until the keyboard pops up.

Delete the default text, then type in a meaningful name for the recording. Hit enter on the on screen keyboard to confirm the name.

# Trim a Memo

You can trim the beginning and the ends of the memo voice recording. To do this, select the recording you want to trim from the list on the left hand side of the main screen. Then tap edit on the top right of the grey panel on the right hand side.

Tap the trim icon on the top right

Now to trim the beginning and ends of the clip, drag the yellow handles along the track until you get to the start and end points you want.

Tap 'trim' when you're done.

# Measure App

The Measure App uses augmented reality to measure distances and objects. I still prefer a good ol' tape measure but let's take a look at the app anyway.

You'll find the Measure App on your home screen.

Point your iPad's camera at the object you want to measure. The Measure App will auto detect any geometric shapes such as the ones on the shelves in the example below. Tap the screen to confirm the detected shape. This will create a mask.

At the edges of the mask, you'll see some small white dots. Tap and drag these to make sure it fully covers the section you want to measure.

Now you can see on the sides of the mask, the Measure App has measured the distances. This particular area is 44cm by 41cm.

You can add points to measure distances between them. To do this, tap the white + icon on the right hand side. You'll see a white dot appear on the screen. Tap the white + icon again to add another point.

Now tap and drag the white points to the edges of the object you want to measure - you'll notice a line will form between them. In the example here, I'm measuring the height of the shelf - so I'm going to drag one point to the top of the shelf, and the other point to the bottom.

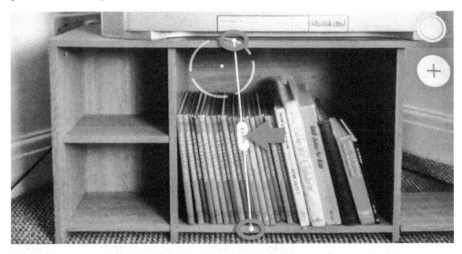

You can see the height of this particular shelf is 43cm. Not 100% accurate yet, the shelf measured to the same points as above with a measuring tape was 49cm, so I wouldn't rely on it if you're doing a bit of DIY.

# Clock App

You can use the clock app to set alarms, timers, as a stop watch, and create time zone clocks so you can see the time in other countries.

You'll find the clock app on your home screen.

## World Clock

With world clock, you can create clocks for any city or country in the world. This is useful if you have friends or family in another country, so you know what time it is there and don't call them in the middle of the night. It's also useful if you're travelling.

To see the world clock, tap 'world clock' on the panel along the bottom of the screen.

To add a clock, tap the + sign on the top right of the screen.

Type in the name of the city or country you want to add

Tap the name of the city/country in the list of suggestions.

Now you'll see the clock appear on the map.

To remove a clock, just tap 'edit' on the top left and you'll see a small red sign appear on the top left of each clock. Tap the red sign to remove it.

## Alarm

You can also set multiple alarms. Eg one for wake up. To do this, select 'alarm' from the panel along the bottom of the screen.

This will display all the alarms you have set.

To set a new alarm, tap the + sign on the top right.

Set the alarm to the time you want the alarm to go off. Tap 'repeat' to set what days you want the alarm, eg 'weekdays'. Tap 'label' to name the alarm, eg 'wakeup'. Tap 'sound' to choose what your alarm sounds like - you can select a sound or a song from your music library. Tap 'save' on the top right when you're done.

You'll see the alarms you've added. Tap the green slider on the alarm to turn in on and off.

# Bed Time

Bed time allows you to create a sleep routine, allowing you to set a time to go to bed and a time to wake up, and the clock app will remind you.

Select 'bed time' from the panel along the bottom of the screen.

The first time you run this feature, you'll need to go through the setup. To do this tap 'get started'. Select the time you want to wake up using the sliders on the screen. Tap 'next'

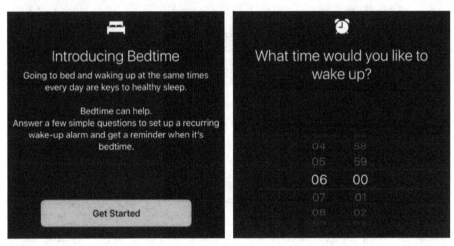

Select the days of the week, then select the number of hours sleep you need. Usually 8 hours. Tap 'next'.

Set the days of the week you want to routine to be in force. Tap 'next'.

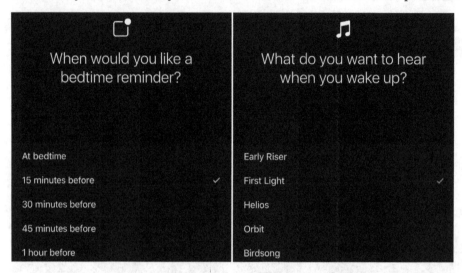

| When would you like a bedtime reminder? | What do you want to hear when you wake up? |
|---|---|
| At bedtime | Early Riser |
| 15 minutes before ✓ | First Light ✓ |
| 30 minutes before | Helios |
| 45 minutes before | Orbit |
| 1 hour before | Birdsong |

Once you've completed the setup, you can see your bedtime on the main screen. To adjust the bedtime time, drag the sleep marker around the clock. Similarly to adjust your wakeup time, drag the wake marker around the clock.

To change your options, tap 'options' on the top left of the screen. Here you can change the days of the week, set a reminder and set a wake up sound.

# Stop Watch

Use the stopwatch to time events. Eg an athletics event. Select 'stopwatch' from the panel along the bottom of the screen.

Tap 'start/stop' to start and stop the timer.

Tap 'lap' to count the number of laps if you are timing a sporting event such as athletics or racing.

# Timer

Use the timer to set a count down timer. Select 'timer' from the panel along the bottom of the screen. Use the sliders to select the length of time in hours, minutes and seconds. For example, if you're playing a game or timing an egg, just set the amount of time allowed.

Tap 'start' to start the count down. Tap the iTunes icon next to where it says 'constellation' to change the sound the timer makes when the time runs out.

# Chapter 7

# Productivity Apps

Apple have developed three productivity apps that allow you to create documents and keynote presentations.

These apps don't usually come pre-installed, so you will need to download them from the app store.

You can do this by searching for 'essentials', then tapping on the 'get' icons for pages and keynote.

# Creating Documents with Pages

To launch Pages, tap the icon on your home screen.

Once Pages 6 has opened, tap 'continue' on the welcome page. If you are launched Pages for the first time, you'll be asked to use iCloud. Click 'Use iCloud'. This enables you to save your documents to your personal cloud space. Next, tap 'create a document'.

You will now need to select a template.

Once you have selected the template to use you will see the main work screen. Let's take a closer look at the main editing screen.

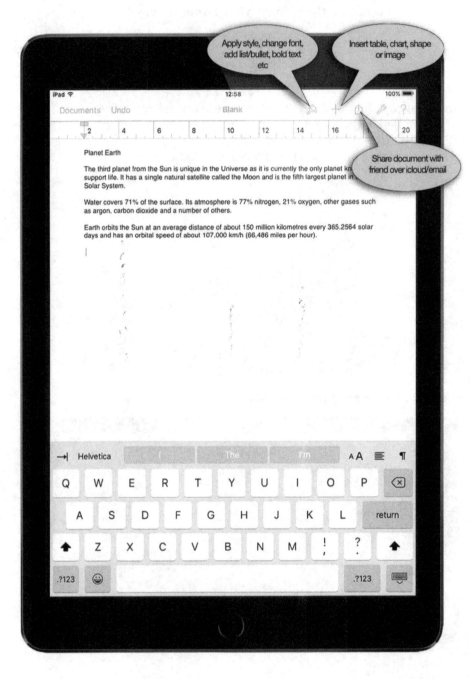

# Formatting Text

Begin typing in your text into the main window as shown above.

The text we entered before needs formatting. To add a heading type it in above the block of text.

Highlight your text with your finger as shown above by dragging the blue dots over the text, then tap the paint brush from the toolbar.

Tap on 'title' to apple the title style to the selected text

Formatting your document means laying it out in a style that is easy to read and looks attractive. This could involve changing fonts, making text bigger for headings, changing colour of text, adding graphics and photographs, etc.

For each document template you choose from the Template Chooser there are a number of pre-set paragraph styles. These are to help you format your document consistently, eg so all headings are the same font, size and colour.

# Adding a Picture

The easiest way to add a picture is to tap the plus sign on the right hand side of the toolbar. Then from the dropdown, tap the image icon on the right. Select one of your albums if you want to insert a photo you took with your camera or tap 'insert from' if you have an image on your iCloud drive. Tap your pictures folder and select an image.

You can resize your image by clicking the resize handles, circled below, and dragging them.

support life. It has a single natural satellite called the Moon and is the fifth largest planet in the Solar System.

You can change the styles by adding borders and shadows by tapping on the paint brush icon on the top right of your toolbar.

# Keynote

Keynote allows you to create multimedia presentations. To launch keynote, go to your home screen and tap keynote.

Tap continue, and if you're running keynote for the first time, tap 'use icloud'.

If you want to create a new presentation, tap 'new document' on the bottom left hand side of the window. From here you can select from a variety of pre-designed templates with different themes, fonts and colours.

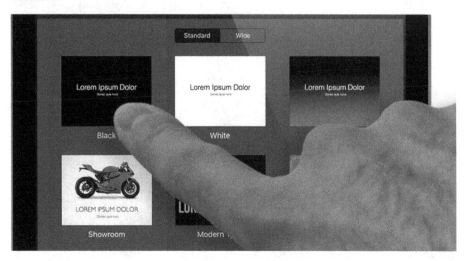

Once you have selected a template you will see the main screen as shown below. This is where you can start building your presentation.

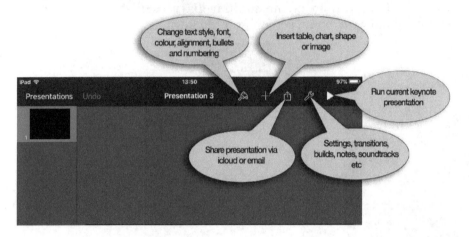

## Editing a Slide

Double tap in the heading field shown below and enter a heading eg 'Planet Earth'. You can tap and drag the heading wherever you like.

## Adding a New Slide

Tap the new slide button located on the bottom left of the screen, then tap a slide layout from the options that appear.

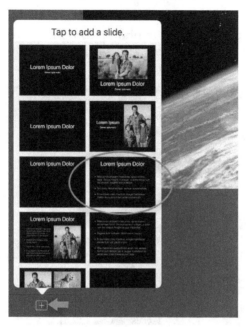

Add some text by double clicking on the text box that appears in the slide.

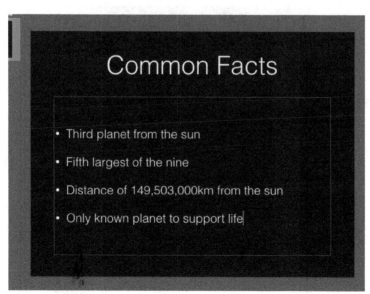

## Adding Media

To add images and media to your slide, tap the plus sign on your tool bar at the top right of your screen. Then tap the image icon on the right.

If you want to add one of your photographs from your photo library, tap on one of your albums and select a photo. If you want to insert a picture from your iCloud, tap 'insert from...'

From your iCloud drive, select pictures. Tap on a picture.

## Animations

Animations allow you to make objects such as text or photographs appear...

Tap on your text box and select the animate icon located on the top right corner of your screen

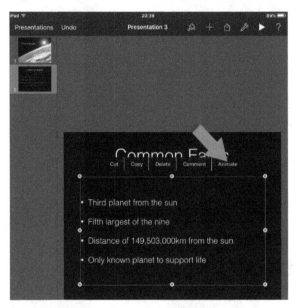

Then tap 'none: build in'

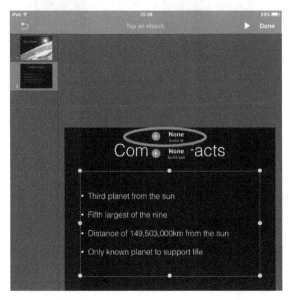

Then select an effect from the effects drop down menu (shown below).

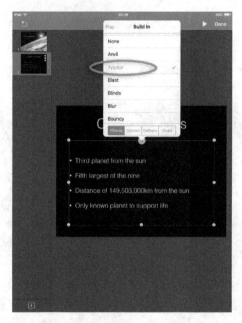

Then specify that you want the bullet points to appear one by one. Tap 'delivery' and select 'by bullet' from the drop down menu.

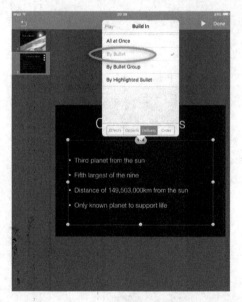

To see what the effect looks like, tap the play button on the top right of your screen.

## Formatting Text Boxes

Tap on a text box you want to format. You can add borders to your text boxes, reflection effects or background colours.

To format the border and fill your text box, tap your text box and tap the paint brush icon, on the top right of the screen.

Tap fill to change the background colour of the text box. Then swipe your finger across the selections of effects and tap on one to select it. In this example, I am going for a nice blue gradient fill.

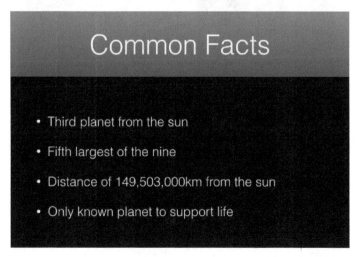

## Formatting Text Inside Textboxes

To change the formatting of the text, for example to change the colour of the text or make it bold.

First select your text in the text box you want to change. Tap on the text three times to select it all. Then tap the paint brush icon on the top right of your toolbar.

From here you can change the font, the font colour, size etc.

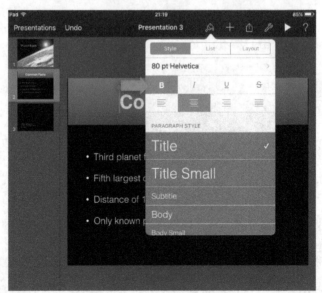

As an example I have changed the colour to light blue and made it bold.

Tap on the font name, illustrated with the red arrow. Then from here I can change the size, the colour and the typeface. You can change these by tapping on the icons down the right.

# Printing Documents

To print documents from an iPad you'll need a printer that is compatible with Air Print. Most modern printers will have this feature included.

## Air Print

If your printer is Air Print enabled, then your printer will show up in the print dialog box automatically.

To print a document, select the share icon, then tap 'print'. If you're using the Pages App, select the '...' icon and tap 'print'.

Select your printer from the printer field, enter the number of copies you want, and select the page range you want to print (eg pages 2-4), or leave it on 'all pages', if you want the whole document.

Tap 'print' on the top right when you're done.

# Older Printers

If your printer doesn't have the Air Print feature, you can download an app from the App Store for your printer.

- **HP Printers** download **HP Smart**

- **Samsung Printers** download **Samsung Mobile Print**

- **Epson Printers** download **Epson iPrint**

- **Canon Printers** download **Canon Print**

Open the app on your iPad and select the document you want to print.

Select print.

# Chapter 8

# Maintaining Your iPad

The new iPads will ship with iOS 12, but if you need to update a previous model then you can do that here.

Apple has dropped support for iPad 2 and the iPhone 4s. iOS 12 will install on the following devices.

- iPad Pro 1st & 2nd generation
- iPad 6th generation
- iPad 5th generation
- iPad Air 2
- iPad Air
- iPad mini 4
- iPad mini 3
- iPad mini 2
- iPhone X, 8, 7, 6, SE, & 5S

Before upgrading, make sure you have some time where you don't need to use your iPad as it will be temporarily inoperative while the installation takes place.

# iPad Backups

You can backup your settings, apps and files to your iCloud account. Go to Settings, Tap on your account name, select 'iCloud', then sign in if you haven't already done so.

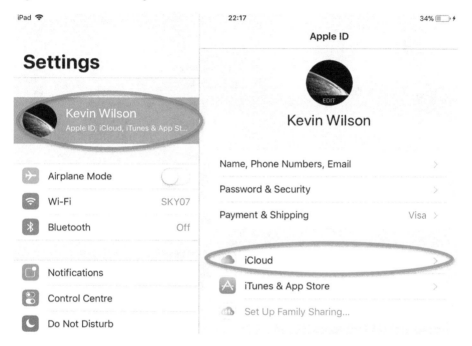

Tap 'Back Up Now'. This is usually the most common way.

*If you use iTunes, plug your device into your computer, select your iPad on the sidebar in iTunes, and select 'Back Up Now'. A backup will then be saved onto your computer's hard disk.*

**257**

# System Updates

To run the update, on your iPad open your settings app. Tap 'general' then select 'Software Update'.

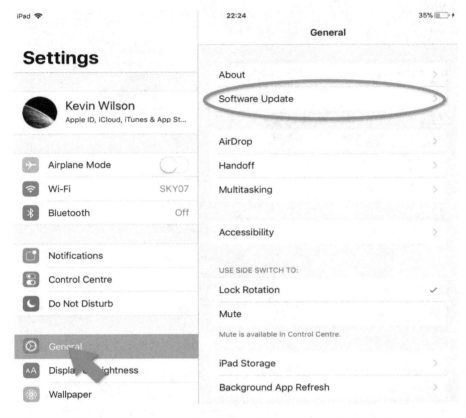

Make sure your device is connected to both Wi-Fi and a power supply, then tap Download and Install to do so.

Depending on your internet connection the installation might take a while.

If you prefer to update using iTunes. Connect your iPad using the cable to a USB port and select your device from the sidebar under devices.

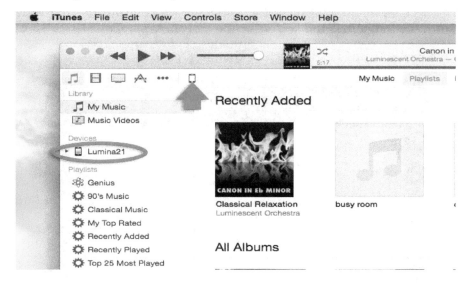

Under Summary, click 'Check for Update', then choose 'Download and Install'.

Confirm your iCloud details.

When updated, your iPad will restart automatically. You may have to run through the initial setup again outlined in chapter 1.

After this, your newly updated device should be ready to use.

# App Updates

To check for app updates, tap the App Store icon on your home screen. From the bar across the bottom of the screen, tap updates.

Any available updates will be listed on this page.

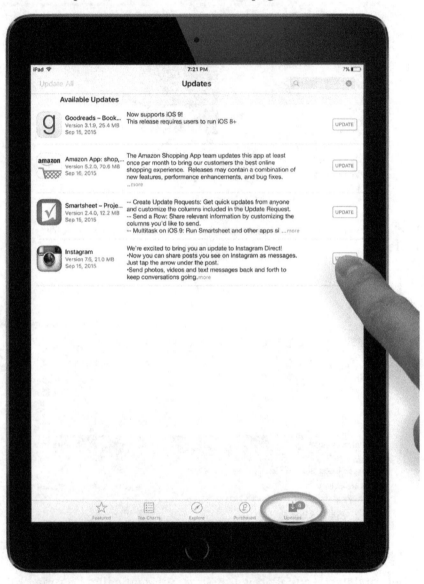

Tap 'update' to update that particular app.

# Deleting Apps

To delete apps, tap and hold your finger on an app, until the X appears on the icon.

Tap on the X to delete the app.

You can also delete any of the pre-installed apps you don't use, in the same way as above.

# iPad Storage Maintenance

This gives you a view of the storage space available on your iPad with some features for freeing up storage space automatically. You can set your iPad to delete move your photos onto the iCloud photo library, empty your 'recently deleted' photos and albums, delete old conversations from iMessage, offload unused apps when your storage runs low and allows you to review large email attachments and messages and whether to keep them or move them off your iPad and onto iCloud.

Open your settings app, tap 'general', then select 'iPad storage'.

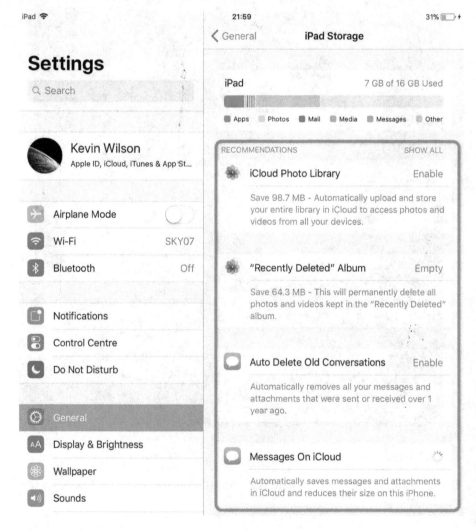

Tap on 'enable' to turn the feature on.

If you scroll further down the list, you'll see a list of individual apps that are currently installed on your iPad. Tap on an app to view details about storage.

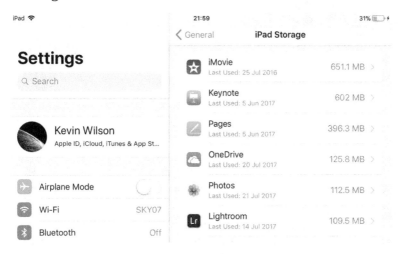

You can manually offload the app. Do this by tapping 'offload app'.

Or you can delete the app. Do this by tapping 'delete app'.

# Chapter 9 Accessorise Your iPad

There are thousands of different accessories available for the iPad and you can buy them from a number of different manufacturers, not only Apple.

You just need to keep in mind the size and model of your iPad when shopping for accessories. Make sure it will fit the model you have; iPad mini, air, pro, etc.

# Smart Keyboards

You can get USB and bluetooth keyboard from a variety of different manufacturers, not just Apple, and make a great little alternative to the on screen keyboard, when you are doing a lot of typing, writing or emailing.

# Cases

A case is a must. You can get hundreds of different types. The ones I find most useful are ones that allow you to stand your iPad up making it great for watching movies. The case folds over covering the screen of the iPad when not in use.

# USB Adapters

These come in useful when you want to connect something to your iPad and most peripherals, if they are not wireless, connect via USB.

These can be keyboards, mice, external hard drives, USB memory sticks, cameras, some models of printers and memory card readers.

# AV Adapters

AV Adapters are useful if you want to connect your iPad to a TV, Monitor or Projector.

You can buy a small adapter that plugs into the port on the bottom of your iPad and will enable you to connect to an HDMI or DVI/VGA connector on your TV or Projector. Most modern TVs and Projectors are HDMI.

DVI

VGA

HDMI

# Power Chargers

You can get a whole range of chargers from all different manufacturers. The most useful ones I have found are the ones that have a powered USB port on the side, that allows you to plug in your iPad and any other tablet for that matter, using the cable that came with.

Your iPad will come with a charger so you won't need to buy one unless you need a replacement.

# Index

# Index

# Index

9 781911 174691